Patrick O'Connell's

Refined American Cuisine

The Inn at Little Washington

Patrick O'Connell's

Refined American Cuisine

The Inn at Little Washington

Photographs by Tim Turner

Bulfinch Press
New York · Boston

January 15, 2009

To Katherine

With Warm Regards,

Patrick O'Connell

See page 232 for additional photo credits.

Bulfinch Press

Time Warner Book Group
1271 Avenue of the Americas, New York, NY 10020
Visit our Web site at www.bulfinchpress.com

First Edition
Second Printing, 2004

Library of Congress Cataloging-in-Publication Data

O'Connell, Patrick.
Patrick O'Connell's refined American cuisine: the Inn at Little Washington / Patrick O'Connell ; photographs by Tim Turner. — 1st ed.
p. cm.
ISBN 0-8212-2845-5
1. Cookery, American. 2. Inn at Little Washington.
I. Inn at Little Washington. II. Title.

TX715.O3225 2004
641.5973 — dc22 2003023018

Design by Trope/Oak Park, Illinois

PRINTED IN THE UNITED KINGDOM

Acknowledgments

છ

T his book could not have come about without the help and inspiration of many individuals to whom I am indebted.

I am grateful to Larry Kirshbaum, chairman and CEO of Time Warner Book Group, who believed in the project and offered his encouragement from the beginning. Thank you to our most frequent guest, Dr. William Raduchel, for introducing me to Larry and helping facilitate our first meeting.

The author at age two and a half. Happily, the baby wasn't thrown out with the bathwater.

out of her culinary degree as we all worked together to tie up the loose ends on time.

I'm grateful to my whole kitchen team at The Inn, especially my hardworking sous chefs, Frank Maragos and Raffaele Dall'Erta, who along with their predecessor, Laurence Gottlieb, assisted with fine-tuning the recipes to ensure that they would turn out in a home kitchen exactly the way we serve them here in the restaurant. Thank you to Mary O'Donnell for testing all the recipes in a home kitchen and for her insightful comments and suggested modifications.

Working with Time Warner Book Group has been a delight, particularly because of the unflagging commitment and enthusiastic support of Jill Cohen, the publisher of Bulfinch Press, and Karen Murgolo, the associate publisher.

A special acknowledgment to my partner and cofounder of The Inn at Little Washington, Reinhardt Lynch, whose vision over the last quarter century has helped keep the ship afloat.

The manuscript might still be unfinished if it weren't for Bonnie Moore, my former sous chef and current projects manager, who kept the book on track while a thousand other things were happening around here and in spite of the fact that after a late night and a couple of chocolate milk shakes, she gave birth several weeks early to a bouncing baby boy. Little William probably became overexcited while tasting all the tantalizing recipes his mommy was sampling.

Thanks to my charming assistant, Rachel Hayden, who jumped into the breach and got some mileage

Tim Turner, the brilliant Chicago food photographer, once again rose to the challenge, somehow managing to surpass his work on my first book (*The Inn at Little Washington Cookbook: A Consuming Passion*). No one can squeeze more glamour out of a plate of food than Tim.

Elizabeth Nelson and Adam Kallish of Trope immersed themselves in the design of the book and managed to convey precisely the tone and feeling this new work demanded.

Thank you to my friend and spiritual advisor, Reverend Richard Emmanuel, who kept candles burning for me in his church in Gloucester, Massachusetts, during dark and uncertain moments throughout the process.

The collective energy of everyone involved created a wonderful momentum that allowed the project to take on a life and identity of its own and emerge from the oven fully baked and ready to devour.

Contents

୧୭

"What are you doing out there?" she demanded. *"It's getting dark!"* *"I'm waiting for my garden to come up,"* I hollered. *"It won't come up. Something's wrong with the seeds."*

Destiny Takes Root

℘

The seeds of my culinary career were planted early but took a long time to bear fruit. When I was about four or five, we moved from an apartment in Washington, D.C., to the dusty little crossroads of Clinton, Maryland, into a house with a little land behind it.

One day, I bought some seed packets with pretty pictures of flowers and vegetables on them and planted my first garden under an apple tree. When dusk came, my mother started calling me for supper. I was still crouched over my garden.

"What are you doing out there?" she demanded. *"It's getting dark!"*

"I'm waiting for my garden to come up," I hollered. *"It won't come up. Something's wrong with the seeds."*

Calmly, she tried to explain that it might take a couple of weeks for the seeds to sprout, and even

longer for the sprouts to become plants, and longer yet for the plants to have flowers and fruit. I unleashed a momentous screaming tantrum: *"I never would have bought the stupid seeds if I'd known that. I'll never plant another garden again as long as I live. Why didn't somebody tell me this before I went to all this trouble?"*

Cleverly, my mother got me to come in by promising that if I would stop screaming, we could make something after dinner that I could enjoy right away — refrigerator cookies. Just slice and bake. They only took twelve minutes to come out of the oven. They were warm and tasted wonderful. Somewhere, a seed must have sprouted that night.

Not surprisingly, my first job at age fifteen was in a restaurant. I would never be able to pass for "normal" again. Just a glimpse into this alluringly addictive subculture was all it took to make me realize that this intensified reality — peopled by the most fascinating and unlikely characters imaginable —

The food on the plate establishes a dialogue with me. Almost immediately, I know the cook's age, his level of culinary training, his exposure to current reference points, the level of palate development, sincerity, sense of humor, and size of ego.

ॐ

was where I belonged. Every day I felt as if I were watching a split-screen film with two shows running simultaneously — the fantasy taking place in the dining room juxtaposed with what was going on behind the scenes in the kitchen.

I went to college to pacify my parents. They had bought into the American dream, believing that their children should never have to toil, sweat, or perform physical labor. In those days, working in a restaurant was considered to be something you did only if you couldn't find a "real" job.

I had planned to become an actor but soon found the "living theater" of the restaurant world more compelling than the stage. I discovered that working with food offered me a much-needed grounding and connection with the real world while satisfying my need for artistic expression.

I have come to realize that like all other art forms, cooking is a vehicle for communication. However, this aspect of the culinary arts is not yet fully understood or appreciated. If you look at a plate of food as a work of art, it can speak volumes. When I contemplate a finished dish, I feel as though I'm seeing it through 3-D glasses, while the rest of the world looks at it with bare eyeballs. Sometimes the plate is telling me more than I want to know.

I usually ask myself, *"What is this dish saying and what is it trying to say?"* Or, more often, *"Who is it pretending to be?"* These are valid and important questions to ask when confronting any work of art.

The food on the plate establishes a dialogue with me. Almost immediately, I know the cook's age, his level of culinary training, his exposure to current reference points, the level of palate development, sincerity, sense of humor, and size of ego. Looking at a plate can exhaust me!

As is the case with any restaurant, a plate of food's success or failure rests on how far short it falls of its intended goal. Honesty and clarity are the two key elements in judging well-prepared food.

I've found it extremely helpful to use musical analogies while critiquing the culinary compositions of young cooks. In order to eliminate "off notes" and bring a dish into balance, I often ask them, *"Who is the star or lead singer in the dish?"* Once that's established, it's easy to point out that the back-up voices are competing or drowning out the featured performer. For example, the tarragon may be overwhelming the chicken, while the lemon may be so subtle that it's "inaudible."

To evolve as a cook, it's essential to critique your work — to ask yourself how a dish might be improved in taste, texture, and appearance. It's helpful to keep a notebook or make notations on your recipes.

I've eaten a lot of my mistakes, as well as some triumphs. Sometimes chefs regret that, unlike the creations of other artists, nothing tangible remains of our work. But we take consolation in the knowledge that memories of the palate can last a lifetime. All of us store them away in the cupboards of our mind and portion them out when needed to provide us with emotional sustenance. They allow us to recall delicious moments in time and remind us that life is worth living.

As cooks we also take pleasure in the knowledge that our art provides nourishment for both the body and the soul. With every meal, a cook is given a blank canvas and another chance to create a masterpiece while savoring the fruits of his labor with others.

And what other artist gets to lick his fingers?

Oddly enough, after all these years I still have trouble answering the seemingly simple question *"What kind of food do you serve in your restaurant?"*

Ruminations on the Title

~ড~

I've heard women say that delivering the second child is always easier, but somehow birthing a second book and choosing an identity for it seemed as laborious as the first. I certainly didn't want a twin or a sequel. There was too much new territory to explore. But, as with my first book, making the connection between what we do in our restaurant and what can be done in a home kitchen has been my foremost goal.

The fact that I taught myself to cook by reading cookbooks (long, long ago) gives me a peculiar advantage over most chefs in my ability to identify with home cooks. The response to my first book, *The Inn at Little Washington Cookbook: A Consuming Passion,* overwhelmed me with encouragement. Years later, I'm still receiving beautiful notes every week from appreciative readers who say that the recipes are easy to follow and produce stunning results. Their encouragement fueled the inspiration for this book.

Oddly enough, after all these years I still have trouble answering the seemingly simple question *"What kind of food do you serve in your restaurant?"* I know all too well that people want an easy one- or two-word label like *Chinese, French,* or *Northern Italian* to which they can attach all of their preconceived biases. At times I've tried dodging the question, somewhat defensively, by explaining that asking such a question is like asking someone to describe his or her personality in one word. My cooking is far more multidimensional. I explain that we try to convey a sense of place at the Inn by making use of the abundance of wonderful products from our region — what the French might call a *cuisine de terroir* — but that we try to elevate these fine, earthy ingredients and use them in unique and interesting new

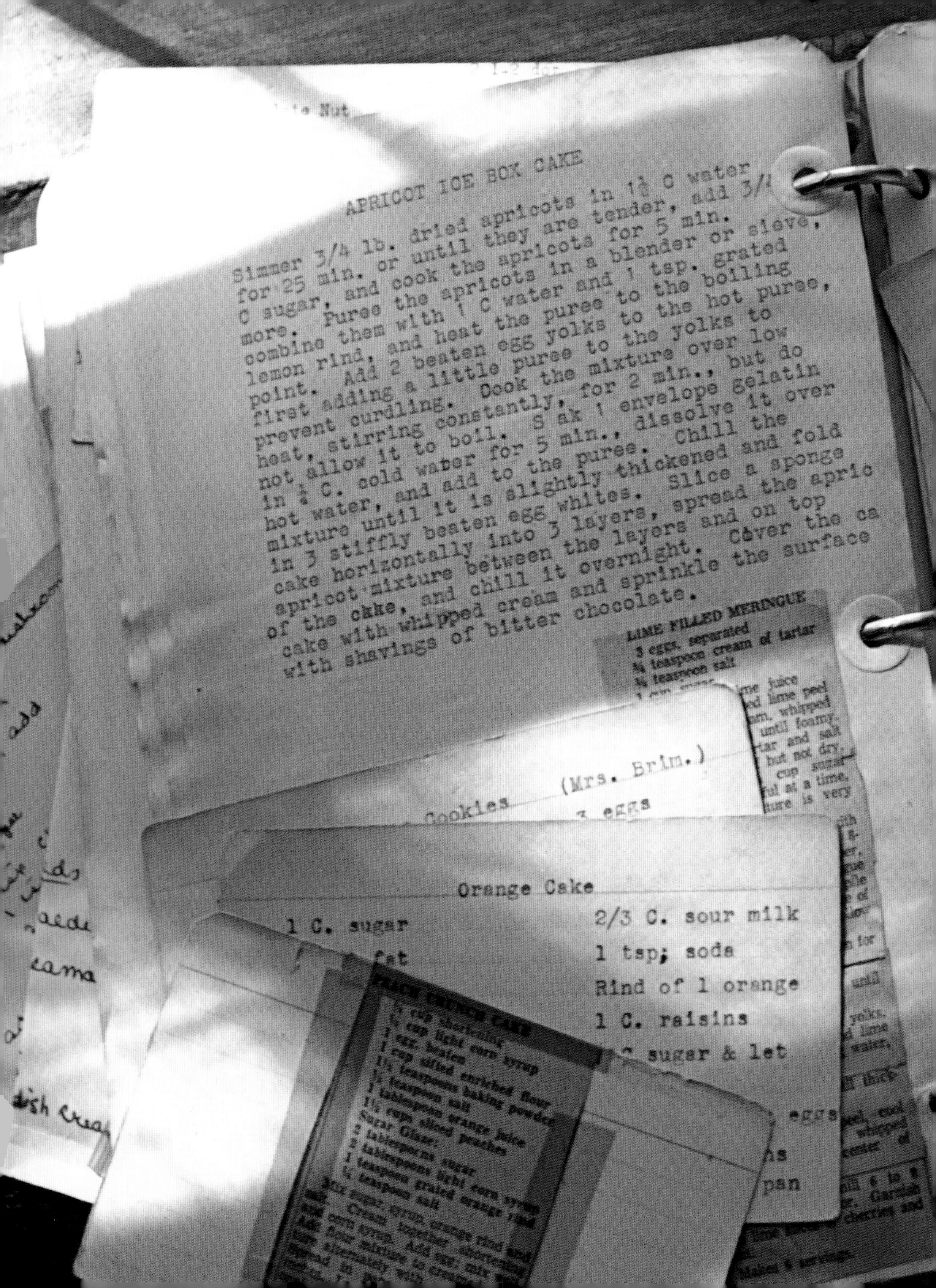

APRICOT ICE BOX CAKE

Simmer 3/4 lb. dried apricots in 1½ C water, add 3/4
for 25 min. or until they are tender, add 3/4
C sugar, and cook the apricots for 5 min.
more.   Puree the apricots in a blender or sieve,
combine them with 1 C water and 1 tsp. grated
lemon rind, and heat the puree to the boiling
point.   Add 2 beaten egg yolks to the hot puree,
first adding a little puree to the yolks to
prevent curdling.   Dook the mixture over low
heat, stirring constantly, for 2 min., but do
not allow it to boil.   Soak 1 envelope gelatin
in ¼ C. cold water for 5 min., dissolve it over
hot water, and add to the puree.   Chill the
mixture until it is slightly thickened and fold
in 3 stiffly beaten egg whites.   Slice a sponge
cake horizontally into 3 layers, spread the apric
apricot mixture between the layers and on top
of the cke, and chill it overnight.   Cover the ca
cake with whipped cream and sprinkle the surface
with shavings of bitter chocolate.

LIME FILLED MERINGUE

3 eggs, separated
¼ teaspoon cream of tartar
¼ teaspoon salt
1 cup sugar

Cookies   (Mrs. Brim.)

3 eggs

Orange Cake

1 C. sugar	2/3 C. sour milk
fat	1 tsp; soda
	Rind of 1 orange
	1 C. raisins
	sugar & let

PEACH CRUNCH CAKE

¼ cup shortening
¼ cup light corn syrup
1 egg, beaten
1 cup oiled
1½ cups sifted enriched flour
½ teaspoons baking powder
½ teaspoon salt
1½ tablespoon orange juice
1½ cups sliced peaches
Sugar Glaze:
3 tablespoons sugar
1 tablespoons light corn syrup
¼ teaspoon grated orange
¼ teaspoon salt

The fact that I taught myself to cook by reading cookbooks (long, long ago) gives me a peculiar advantage over most chefs in my ability to identify with home cooks.

℘

ways while still preserving the soulful flavors and memories we associate with them.

As an American cooking with American products, it would seem straightforward and accurate to simply call my cooking "American" and be done with it. But to this day, American cooking still conjures up notions of the simple, rustic foods of our grandmothers, or worse, the mundane home cooking of the fifties, when convenience first became mistaken for luxury.

It has taken me a long time to realize that what I've been doing over the last quarter century at the Inn at Little Washington is evolving and refining many of the dishes I grew up with, making them relevant to a new century while keeping their soul intact — building a sort of culinary bridge between the past and future.

In an attempt to identify a new dimension of American cuisine, pioneered by a new breed of American chefs, food journalists in the eighties labeled what we were doing as "New American" cuisine. While the label helped create a distinction from what had gone before, it was too broad to accurately describe how far professional cooking in the United States had evolved.

In France, an age-old distinction is drawn between everyday home cooking and what is referred to as "haute cuisine" — the grand art of the great chefs. For the first time in America's history, it is time to draw a parallel distinction. A new terminology is needed.

I am comfortable with a label that appropriately defines my cooking and accurately describes our country's equivalent to French haute cuisine — and it's only three words — *refined American cuisine.*

Less than twenty-five years ago, using the adjective *refined* in conjunction with American cooking would have constituted an oxymoron. But in this relatively short period of time in our country's brief culinary history, an amazing acceleration has occurred. Seemingly overnight, the best of our nation's restaurants are now on a par with the finest anywhere in the world. The profile of the American chef has changed dramatically, and there has been a 180-degree turn in the status attached to the culinary profession. The American restaurant audience is no longer easily intimidated or impressed by pretension. A new confidence has replaced previous insecurities about dining. As a culture, we have become food savvy to the point of jadedness.

As a self-taught chef I know that many of the tricks, techniques, and shortcuts that I use every day in the restaurant lend themselves perfectly to the home kitchen. I am confident that with these recipes you can produce dazzling and delicious meals for your family and guests without spending all day in the kitchen. Most of my favorite dishes are the simplest and depend on a few ingredients of the finest quality. I like food to appear effortless in its presentation — as though it dropped on the plate from the sky or was blown onto it by a gentle breeze — never touched by human hands, or stacked and tortured as was the trend for a while.

Hopefully this book will inspire you to rethink some of your favorite American classics and cherished family recipes and update them for today's tastes. With a bit of creative refinement, traditional dishes can become surprisingly chic and still do your ancestors proud. If our grandmothers had only realized that you don't always have to suffer to cook beautifully there might have been a little less guilt in the world.

After attending an event at somebody else's place, guests always critiqued the party on the way home, and its success was judged on how much the hostess had fussed. I came to understand that homemaking was a competitive art.

Entertaining Thoughts

ളᎧ

As a kid growing up in a large, Irish-Catholic family in the era of Ozzie and Harriet, I always assumed that the only reason people entertained was to have an incentive to clean their house.

My mother would begin scrubbing weeks before guests were scheduled to arrive, working room by room — sealing off each room after it passed the white-glove test.

A path of newspapers would be laid down throughout the house, and no one was allowed to step off it. The kitchen cabinets were emptied and scoured. All the canned goods and McCormick spices were washed, dried, and arranged alphabetically. On the last day of the countdown, all the windows were washed inside and out, and on the day of the party, the bathroom was given a sterilizing makeover, after which boys were instructed to use the woods until the company had left.

Monogrammed linen hand towels that no one ever used were hung on the towel racks. Everybody, including the guests, understood that those towels were never supposed to be touched. They were there to establish our rank in the social order of things. No one was ever surprised when they were returned to the linen closet unused after every party. My brother explained to me that men were supposed to use their socks to dry their hands, but I was never quite sure what the women did. They were always so clever; I suspected they carried a little towel in their purse for such occasions.

By the time all the children were either dressed and scrubbed or hidden and my mother had done her makeup, we were all wiped out — but that was one clean house. The arrival of the guests was totally anticlimactic. We couldn't wait for them to leave. We were always exhausted.

When my grandmother came for a visit, the program would go into overdrive. Even the attic got cleaned, which was odd because Grandma could never have climbed the retractable ladder, or "vanishing staircase" as it was called, and gone up there to inspect it.

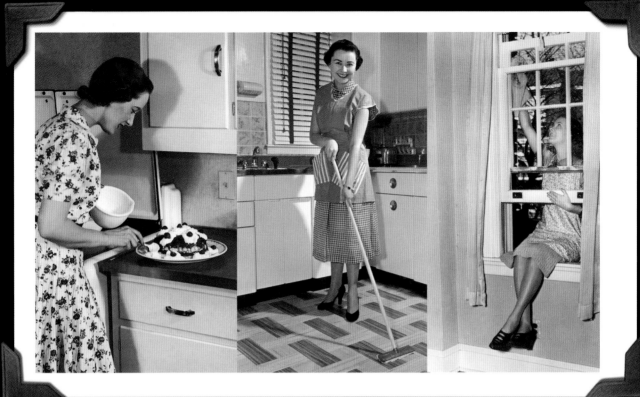

Ever since I opened the Inn at Little Washington in 1978 with my partner, Reinhardt Lynch, we've never really thought of it as a restaurant — just a hideaway in the country owned by two people who like to entertain a lot. For more than twenty-six years it has felt as if we've been hosting one continuous house party.

&

In my mother's circle, ladies would respond with a kind of coded message whenever they were invited over. They'd always say, *"Now don't go to any fuss, dear."* I learned to interpret that to mean that it wouldn't be necessary to repaint the house.

One day while a friend and I were bragging about how weird our families were, he confessed that his mother took bathroom cleaning a step further and did it the same way Tina Turner recorded "What's Love Got to Do with It" — buck naked. Naturally, we thought he was putting us on, until he invited us over to watch through the keyhole. Sure enough, she was locked in there with nothing on but her Babbo cleanser, singing and dancing around. We thought she actually gave Tina Turner a pretty good

run for her money. It was comforting to know there were mothers who were even more passionate about cleanliness than my own.

After attending an event at somebody else's place, guests always critiqued the party on the way home, and its success was judged on how much the hostess had fussed. I came to understand that homemaking was a competitive art. At about this time, I began to realize that almost everything in our culture was backward and that it would probably make a lot more sense to clean the house *after* you had a party. At least you'd have more energy to put into the food.

Party food of that era was also intended to look fussed over. No matter how hard I try I will never be

able to forget what today would be called my mother's "signature dish." It was called "Little Nancy Etticoat in Her White Petticoat" and was apparently inspired by an obscure nursery rhyme about a candle. It was a banana coming straight up through a Dole pineapple ring, surrounded by a chiffonade of iceberg lettuce, with a dollop of Hellmann's mayonnaise dripping down the sides — capped off by a Maraschino cherry — definitely a conversation stopper.

The Little Nancy salads would be already placed on the table before we sat down. Guests would stare with wide-eyed wonderment, never knowing quite what to say. One of the women, obviously at a loss for words but needing to fill the silence, would usually murmur: *"Oh, Gwen!"* (my mother's name is Gwendolyn). That would be her cue to chime right in and recite the nursery rhyme: *"Little Nancy Etticoat in her white petticoat. The longer she stands, the shorter she grows."* A respectful pause followed while the guests contemplated the best way of addressing the dish with knife and fork. For a small child whose chin barely reached the table, that salad had a rather haunting, larger-than-life aspect to it. Mysteriously, when my brothers and I began to reach puberty, the Little Nancy Etticoat salad disappeared from my mother's entertaining repertoire. Maybe good bananas just became hard to come by in Clinton — I never asked her. All I can say is, that's a dish I've never had the balls to serve.

Ever since I opened the Inn at Little Washington in 1978 with my partner, Reinhardt Lynch, we've never really thought of it as a restaurant — just a hide-away in the country owned by two people who like to entertain a lot. For more than twenty-six years it has felt as if we've been hosting one continuous house party. Sometimes it seems like a Broadway show that won't quit — calamities happen every day, but somehow the show still opens every night.

I'll always remember one summer afternoon years ago when I answered the phone in the kitchen and an incoherent farmer, who must have had a chaw of tobacco in his mouth, was trying to sell me something. Finally, I was able to make out that he had some blueberries. I kept asking how many he had, but couldn't understand his response. I suggested he just come on by with the berries. About twenty minutes later, a dusty pickup overflowing with crates and boxes of giant blueberries pulled up to the kitchen door. I had never seen so many blueberries in my life. They were spilling out all over the place, bursting with succulence and almost the size of eyeballs.

I complimented his berries and told him I could take two or three boxes. He hit the roof and hollered: *"You promised you'd take 'em all. You told me to bring 'em all up here."* I hemmed and hawed and noticed the big vein pulsing in his neck. Then he said, *"My son's in the hospital. Got hit in the head*

As I ran toward the back room, blueberries began pouring through the doorway like lava from an erupting volcano.

ℰ☯

with a baseball bat. You gotsta take 'em all." I looked into the bed of the pickup and saw a whole mountain of blueberries staring me down. Then I heard myself say, *"Okay, I'll take them all."*

That summer I had a very tiny young woman named Debbie assisting me in the kitchen. She was not *technically* a dwarf, but with her pigtails she could easily pass for an eleven-year-old girl. Deb was quick and fearless behind the line. Because she couldn't reach the broiler, we improvised a platform for her to stand on made out of two wooden Coke crates. She took up so little space that when we were busy she could position herself right between my feet. Her head came up to my waist, and we were able to work together like a creature with four arms.

I paid the farmer twenty-six dollars and asked Debbie to give him a hand unloading the blueberries. We quickly filled what little refrigeration space we had in our kitchen and began stacking the berries in an unfinished back room where someone had left a little old household refrigerator. After the farmer departed, I decided I'd better get busy working those blueberries into the evening's menu and began to make a big batch of blueberry ice cream. I asked Deb to go in the back and bring out a box of the berries, while I started the ice cream custard base. As I was whisking the egg yolks, I heard a blood-curdling scream. I froze, thinking surely somebody must be dead. As I ran toward the back room, blueberries began pouring through the doorway like lava from an erupting volcano. I was knee deep in them before I saw the old Admiral refrigerator lying on top of poor Debbie. Apparently, she and the farmer had stacked boxes of berries on top of it, and when she pulled the door open, the whole thing fell forward, dumping its contents on top of her. It looked like a train wreck as I lifted the little refrigerator off of her. She was black and mostly blue, but miraculously unharmed because gallons of blueberries had cushioned the weight of the refrigerator. I was

relieved when she hopped up and cussed me out. Only her pride had been wounded.

The next thing I focused on was my poor blueberries. They could not go to waste. We hosed Debbie off and began scooping up the berries. My conscience prevented me from making them into ice cream, but after a good wash I realized that I could at least make blueberry vinegar. After all, no germs could live in vinegar.

The next hurdle was figuring out how to use twenty gallons of blueberry vinegar. That's when inspiration struck and my Charcoal-Grilled Poussin Marinated in Blueberry Vinegar was born. What a great dish it turned out to be! The vinegar had a tenderizing effect on the poultry, tinted the flesh an exotic shade of blue, and caused the skin to become wonderfully crisp and crackly. It still appears on the menu every summer.

The tabletops were sprinkled with flower petals, strewn with colorful seed packets, and scattered with ground Oreo cookies, which looked in every way like dirt.

ॐ

Sometimes little disasters provide educational and creative opportunities.

Over the years, I've learned that being obsessive-compulsive can be a helpful attribute for successful entertaining. Rather than consider it a neurosis, I choose to regard obsessiveness simply as the capacity to block out everything but one idea or thought process, and when you're doing something as intense as giving a party, you shouldn't be thinking about anything else anyway. There are too many details to consider.

No detail emphasizes the exquisite pleasure of an ephemeral moment at the table more perfectly than flowers. Arranging them should be fun — not intimidating. They need not be expensive — just unique. For example, freshly cut bunches of herbs in little antique crocks might have more impact than a costly arrangement. As with the food, they should relate to the time of year and the occasion. It's important to keep flowers understated and in scale with their surroundings. I teach our staff to think of a table setting or a buffet as if it were a still-life painting — fluid, soft, and moody.

I like to serve each course on a different china pattern relative to the food being served and have actually been known to create a meal around pieces of china I couldn't resist buying. The most ordinary-looking dish can often be transformed by presenting it on a stunning, complementary plate.

I believe in introducing a bit of whimsy when setting a table. For example, when we prepared the late James Beard's ninety-ninth birthday dinner in New York, I wanted to bring the feeling of springtime in the country to the city. On each table, enormous branches of flowering cherry trees in tall vases made

the guests feel as if they were dining in a cherry orchard. The tabletops were sprinkled with flower petals, strewn with colorful seed packets, and scattered with ground Oreo cookies, which looked in every way like dirt. Tiny morel mushrooms, bits of moss, weathered garden gloves, and artificial insects completed the woodland fairy tale. The setting created a relaxed and amusing tone at the outset of the evening and gave the guests plenty to talk about as they traded seed packets and built up enough courage to eat "dirt." A little unexpected humor is always welcome.

While planning a party, it's a good exercise to ask yourself what will be remembered most by your guests long after the party is over. More often than not, it's the tiniest personal touches that reflect who you are. After all, entertaining is simply about sharing your private world with others. What could be more fascinating than a glimpse into another person's reality or fantasy. We often refer to *our* world as "fantality" — halfway between fantasy and reality.

I'm always advising cooks and culinary students to develop reference points by going to great restaurants and keeping a little notebook of ideas and comments to refer to later. The same idea works for someone who takes entertaining seriously. A party notebook full of ideas you've gleaned over the years can be invaluable when you find yourself planning a special event.

A successful party, like a great film or work of art, elevates the spirit, makes people feel life is worth living, and enhances a guest's self-esteem. We should entertain more often! How else are we ever going to get the house clean?

Breakfast

ℂ

Rösti Potatoes with Smoked Salmon and Scrambled Eggs

In Switzerland, rösti *means "crisp and golden." The word has become synonymous with the country's famous potato cake. The potato cake makes a delicious cushion for ribbons of smoked salmon and lightly scrambled eggs. Simply finished with a sprinkling of capers, diced red onion, chives, and dill, this dish is a lighter and more interesting brunch selection than the usual eggs Benedict and allows you to feel virtuous because you didn't consume the unneeded calories in a hollandaise sauce.*

✿

Serves 6

Rösti Potatoes

2 large Idaho potatoes

Salt and freshly ground white pepper
   to taste

½ cup clarified butter

Scrambled Eggs

12 eggs

3 tablespoons crème fraîche

Salt and freshly ground white pepper
   to taste

To Serve and Garnish

12 slices smoked salmon

2 tablespoons crème fraîche

2 teaspoons capers

2 teaspoons finely diced red onion

2 teaspoons finely chopped
   fresh chives

2 teaspoons chopped fresh dill

To Make the Rösti Potatoes

1. Peel the potatoes and steam them for 15 minutes. Let cool.

2. Using the large-holed blade of a box grater, shred the potatoes.

3. Season the shredded potatoes with salt and white pepper and form them into 6 cakes.

4. In a large skillet, heat half of the clarified butter over medium heat. Carefully place 3 cakes in the skillet and brown them on both sides for about 5 to 7 minutes per side. Remove and drain on paper towels. Repeat with the remaining clarified butter and potato cakes. (The rösti potatoes can be made up to 1 hour in advance and rewarmed before serving.)

To Make the Scrambled Eggs

1. In the top of a double boiler or in a stainless steel bowl that will rest securely on top of a pot of simmering water, whisk together the eggs, crème fraîche, salt, and pepper.

2. Place the mixture over a pot of simmering water and stir, folding the eggs with a rubber spatula until they are very lightly scrambled.

To Serve and Garnish

1. Place one warm rösti potato in the center of each plate.

2. Form two slices of salmon into circular ribbons on top of each rösti potato.

3. Place a spoonful of scrambled eggs on top of the smoked salmon and garnish the eggs with a small dollop of crème fraîche. Sprinkle with capers, red onion, chives, and dill.

Grown-up Oatmeal Soufflés

The word soufflé *literally translates as "breath." This recipe will not only breathe new life into a bowl of porridge but also strike your guests as a breath of fresh air. All of the nourishing, comforting memories of the oatmeal you grew up with are preserved and raised to new heights in this unique and ethereal presentation.*

The soufflé comprises two layers. Regular sweetened oatmeal is placed on the bottom of the dish, and a delicate oatmeal soufflé batter is poured on top, allowing the soufflé to rise easily while still retaining the homespun texture of porridge.

ℰℭ

To Prepare the Soufflé Molds

Butter the insides of 8 eight-ounce ramekins and sprinkle them with sugar.

To Prepare the Sweetened-Oatmeal Bottom Layer

1. In a stainless steel saucepan, bring the heavy cream and milk to a boil. Stir in the oats and boil for 5 minutes. Stir in the sugar and maple syrup.

2. Remove from heat and pour ¼ cup of the sweetened oatmeal into each ramekin. Reserve the remaining sweetened oatmeal (you should have about ¾ cup left) for the soufflé layer.

To Prepare the Soufflé Layer

1. Preheat the oven to 375 degrees.

2. In a spice grinder or small food processor, grind the oats until they resemble coarse meal.

3. In a 4-quart stainless steel saucepan, melt the butter over medium heat. Stir in the ground oats and flour and cook, stirring, for 30 seconds.

4. Slowly whisk the milk into the flour mixture and bring to a boil. Add the reserved sweetened oatmeal and stir until combined. Turn heat to low. Stir in ½ cup sugar, the maple syrup, and the rum.

5. In a small bowl, whisk the cornstarch into the egg yolks and add to the saucepan. Whisk constantly and remove from heat just before the mixture comes to a boil. Let cool slightly.

6. In the bowl of an electric mixer, begin whisking the egg whites on low speed until they become frothy. Increase the speed to high and add the remaining 3 tablespoons of sugar in a steady stream. Continue whipping until the egg whites form medium-stiff peaks.

7. Stir a small portion of the egg whites into the cooled oatmeal mixture, then fold in the remaining egg whites. Pour the soufflé mixture on top of the sweetened-oatmeal bottom layer in the ramekins.

8. Place the filled ramekins on a baking sheet and place it in the center of the oven. Bake for about 15 to 20 minutes, or until the soufflés are just set and light golden brown.

To Serve

As soon as the soufflés come out of the oven, serve them with maple syrup and rum-soaked currants on the side.

Serves 8

For the Soufflé Molds

3 tablespoons soft butter

4 tablespoons sugar

Sweetened-Oatmeal Bottom Layer

1¾ cups heavy cream

1½ cups milk

1¾ cups instant oats

3 tablespoons sugar

3 tablespoons maple syrup

Soufflé Layer

¼ cup instant oats

2 tablespoons butter

1 tablespoon all-purpose flour

1¾ cups milk

¾ cup sweetened oatmeal (reserved from previous recipe)

½ cup plus 3 tablespoons sugar

¼ cup maple syrup

1 tablespoon dark rum

½ teaspoon cornstarch

3 egg yolks

12 egg whites

Garnishes

Maple syrup

Currants soaked in dark rum (optional)

Cottage Cheese and Buttermilk Pancakes with Peach-Fig Syrup

Cottage cheese adds a rich flavor and creamy texture to these light and airy pancakes. They can be served with a variety of seasonal fruit accompaniments. Our guests are particularly fond of the peach-fig syrup.

Serves 6

Peach-Fig Syrup

1½ tablespoons butter

1½ cups peeled, pitted, and sliced peaches

1 cup quartered figs, preferably Black Mission

½ cup maple syrup

Pancakes

1 cup cottage cheese

2 cups all-purpose flour

¼ cup sugar

½ teaspoon baking soda

2 teaspoons baking powder

1 teaspoon salt

2 eggs

1½ cups buttermilk

1½ tablespoons butter, melted

1 tablespoon grated lemon zest

Nonstick cooking spray

To Make the Peach-Fig Syrup

1. In a 10-inch skillet over medium heat, melt the butter. Add the peaches and figs and cook for about 2 minutes, stirring constantly, until the mixture comes to a simmer.

2. Add the maple syrup, bring to a boil, and cook for 2 minutes more. (This syrup may be made well in advance and rewarmed before serving.)

To Make the Pancakes

1. Preheat the oven to 250 degrees.

2. Place a sieve over a bowl, add the cottage cheese to the sieve, and drain off the excess liquid.

3. In a mixing bowl, combine the flour, sugar, baking soda, baking powder, and salt.

4. In a separate bowl, whisk the eggs, buttermilk, drained cottage cheese, butter, and lemon zest together. Fold in the flour mixture.

5. Spray a griddle or large skillet with nonstick cooking spray and heat it over medium heat. Spoon a heaping tablespoon of batter onto the griddle for each pancake. Cook until golden brown, about 2 minutes, then turn the pancake over and cook for about 1 more minute. Keep the pancakes warm in the oven until ready to serve.

6. Serve the pancakes with the peach-fig syrup.

Swanky and Cheesy Shrimp and Grits

Nothing makes for a more soul-satisfying Southern-style Sunday brunch than sweet shrimp and creamy grits. The unexpected addition of the mascarpone cheese adds a subtle richness to the earthy, coarsely ground cornmeal. The Roasted Tomato and Shallot Fondue is reminiscent of another breakfast staple in the repertoire of Southern comfort food — stewed tomatoes.

ࡇ

To Make the Grits

1. In a 2-quart saucepan, bring the water to a boil.
2. Slowly whisk in the grits. Simmer over low heat, stirring occasionally, until the grits are soft and creamy, about 20 to 30 minutes.
3. Stir in the mascarpone cheese, heavy cream, Roasted Garlic, salt, pepper, and sugar and cook for 2 or 3 more minutes.
4. Keep warm until ready to use.

For the Shrimp

1. In a large skillet, heat the olive oil over medium-high heat. Add the shrimp and sauté for 3 minutes, or until they are just pink, being careful not to overcook. Add the garlic and sauté for a few seconds more.
2. Add the wine or vermouth, Roasted Tomato and Shallot Fondue, and scallions and simmer briefly. Add the butter and season with salt and pepper.

To Serve

Mound the grits in the center of each bowl. Spoon the shrimp and tomato mixture on the center of the grits.

Serves 6

Grits

4 cups water

1 cup grits, preferably good-quality stone-ground organic

1½ tablespoons mascarpone cheese

¼ cup heavy cream

1 tablespoon Roasted Garlic (see page 217)

Salt and freshly ground black pepper to taste

Pinch of sugar

Shrimp

1 tablespoon olive oil

1½ pounds large shrimp, peeled, deveined, and halved

¼ teaspoon minced garlic

¼ cup dry white wine or vermouth

1 cup Roasted Tomato and Shallot Fondue (see page 217)

2 tablespoons chopped scallions

1 tablespoon butter

Salt and freshly ground black pepper to taste

Bourbon Pecan Waffles

Bourbon, buttermilk, and pecans give these waffles a deep Southern accent and a luscious taste and texture. Our favorite way to serve them is simply with pecan halves cooked in a little butter, bourbon, and maple syrup. Your guests just might be drawlin' for more.

Makes about 8 waffles

Pecan-Butter Syrup

½ pound (2 sticks) butter

I cup pecan halves

I cup maple syrup

¼ cup bourbon

Waffles

Nonstick cooking spray

2 eggs, separated

I cup all-purpose flour

I cup chopped pecans

2 tablespoons sugar

¼ pound (I stick) butter, melted

½ cup bourbon

I teaspoon vanilla extract

2 teaspoons baking powder

1½ cups buttermilk

½ cup crème fraîche (for garnish)

To Make the Pecan-Butter Syrup

1. In a 10-inch skillet over medium heat, melt the butter. Add the pecan halves. Cook for about 3 minutes, stirring constantly, until the pecans are well toasted and lightly colored.

2. Just as the butter begins to foam, pour in the maple syrup.

3. Remove the skillet from the heat and carefully add the bourbon. Return to heat and cook the mixture for 1 more minute. This syrup may be made well in advance and rewarmed before serving.

To Make the Waffles

1. Spray a waffle iron with nonstick cooking spray and preheat it. Preheat the oven to 200 degrees.

2. In a mixing bowl, whip the egg whites to medium-stiff peaks.

3. Combine the egg yolks, flour, pecans, sugar, butter, bourbon, vanilla extract, baking powder, and buttermilk in a food processor and mix until smooth. Transfer this mixture to a large mixing bowl and fold in the egg whites.

4. With a ladle, fill the waffle iron with batter and cook until the waffle is golden brown, about 8 minutes. Place the waffle on a wire rack on a baking sheet and keep warm in the oven. Continue in the same manner until all the batter is used.

5. Serve the waffles with pecan-butter syrup and a dollop of crème fraîche.

Shenandoah Sunrise Cocktail

This is our version of a champagne cocktail made with blood oranges. Once rarely grown outside of Sicily, these sweet, ruby-fleshed oranges are now widely raised in the state of California and are in season from November through March. This brunch drink can be made with or without champagne. We combine blood-orange juice with freshly squeezed orange or tangelo juice so that the color of the drink resembles a sunrise.

℘

Serves 6

Cocktail

¼ cup freshly squeezed tangelo juice (orange juice may be substituted)

¼ cup freshly squeezed blood-orange juice

¼ cup Drambuie liqueur (optional)

I bottle chilled champagne

Virgin Shenandoah Sunrise

I cup freshly squeezed blood-orange juice

6 cups freshly squeezed tangelo juice (orange juice may be substituted)

To Make the Cocktail

1. In a small pitcher, combine the tangelo and blood-orange juice.

2. Divide the juice mixture and Drambuie among 6 champagne glasses and fill the remainder of the glasses with champagne.

To Make a Virgin Shenandoah Sunrise

Divide the blood-orange juice among 6 tall, stemmed glasses and fill the remainder of the glasses with tangelo juice.

Peach-Vanilla Jam

Because peach season is always too short, we look for ways to enjoy this luscious fruit from our local orchards all year long. The unexpected fragrance of vanilla bean adds a pleasantly surprising nuance to the wonderful flavor of fresh peaches in this chunky, old-fashioned jam. We prefer to use a grated apple for its natural pectin to thicken the jam, making it less stiff than jams made with commercial pectin.

Makes 3 cups

1 Granny Smith apple

4 cups peeled, pitted, and sliced peaches

1¾ cups sugar

2 tablespoons lemon juice

1 vanilla bean, split lengthwise

1. Using a grater, grate the apple, including the skin and core, but not the seeds.

2. In a heavy-bottomed saucepan, combine the grated apple, peaches, sugar, and 1 tablespoon of the lemon juice and cook over low heat until the fruit begins to soften.

3. Add the vanilla bean and simmer the preserves, stirring frequently and skimming any foam that rises to the surface. Cook until the mixture registers 220 degrees on a candy thermometer. Remove from heat.

4. Stir in the remaining lemon juice and cool to room temperature.

5. Pour the jam into sterile glass jars or airtight storage containers and chill until ready to serve. The vanilla bean may be left in the jam to allow the vanilla flavor to intensify. For longer storage, the jam can be frozen.

Jellied Melon Parfaits

This is a simple, elegant do-ahead breakfast or brunch dish that can be modified according to whatever fruit is in season. Very ripe melons are pureed, strained, and combined with a little gelatin. When set, the fruit jelly is layered alternately with plain yogurt and fresh berries to create a healthy, colorful parfait.

To Make the Melon Jelly

1. Puree the melon in a food processor. Strain the puree through a sieve into the top of a double boiler or into a large stainless steel bowl.
2. Sprinkle the gelatin over the melon puree. When the gelatin has softened, set the mixture over a pot of simmering water and stir until the gelatin has completely dissolved and the mixture registers 180 degrees on a candy thermometer.
3. Stir in the lemon juice. Cover and refrigerate for several hours until set.

To Make the Parfaits

1. Carefully pour 2 tablespoons of yogurt into the bottom of each of 6 parfait or stemmed glasses.
2. Spoon 2 tablespoons of melon jelly on top of the yogurt.
3. Layer another 2 tablespoons of yogurt on top of the jelly. Sprinkle a few raspberries on top of the yogurt. Spoon 2 more tablespoons of yogurt on top of the raspberries.
4. Spoon 2 more tablespoons of jelly over the yogurt.
5. Finish each parfait with 2 more tablespoons of yogurt. The parfaits may be assembled, covered, and kept overnight in the refrigerator.

Serves 6

Melon Jelly

2 small or 1 large, ripe melon, peeled, seeded, and chopped (enough to yield 2 cups of puree)

2 teaspoons unflavored gelatin powder

Juice of 1 lemon

Parfaits

3 cups plain yogurt

1 recipe melon jelly

1 cup fresh raspberries

Snacks and Canapés

80

Sole Fingers with Green Herb Mayonnaise

Like many good Catholic families, we always ate Mrs. Paul's fish sticks on Friday night when I was growing up. I still remember them fondly. Perhaps it was a fit of nostalgia that inspired this whimsical look-alike.

The French call these crispy strips of fish goujonettes. *We have nicknamed them "sole fingers." No matter what you call them, they are fun to make and irresistible to nibble. In the restaurant, we serve them on a bed of Crispy Collard Greens (which looks like seaweed) and accompany them with a green herb mayonnaise.*

છ

For the Green Herb Mayonnaise

1. Combine all of the ingredients in a food processor and puree until smooth.
2. Strain through a fine mesh sieve and store in the refrigerator until needed.

For the Sole Fingers

1. In a deep fryer or heavy pot, heat the oil to 350 degrees.
2. Combine the cornmeal, salt, and pepper in a shallow bowl.
3. Place the buttermilk in a small bowl and soak the strips of sole in it for 5 minutes. Drain the fish well and lightly coat it in the seasoned cornmeal, shaking off any excess. The fish may be prepared in advance to this point and kept refrigerated for several hours.
4. Carefully drop the sole fingers one by one into the hot oil and fry for about 1 minute, turning them with a slotted spoon until they are golden brown.
5. Remove the fish from the fryer and drain on paper towels. Season with salt and serve on Crispy Collard Greens (if desired) with green herb mayonnaise on the side.

Serves 4

Green Herb Mayonnaise

2 tablespoons capers, drained

¼ cup tightly packed fresh dill, stems removed

¼ cup tightly packed fresh Italian parsley, stems removed

¼ cup tightly packed watercress, stems removed

2 tablespoons tarragon leaves

1 tablespoon Dijon mustard

2 teaspoons fresh lemon juice

½ teaspoon kosher salt

Freshly ground black pepper to taste

1 cup good-quality mayonnaise, preferably homemade

Sole Fingers

2 quarts vegetable or peanut oil (for deep-frying)

2 cups cornmeal

1 tablespoon salt

½ teaspoon freshly ground black pepper

1 cup buttermilk

12 ounces Dover sole, lemon sole, or flounder, cut into 3-inch strips (about the thickness of a finger)

1 recipe Crispy Collard Greens (optional, see page 212)

1 recipe green herb mayonnaise

Miniature Ham Biscuits with Mascarpone Pepper Jelly

Nobody who visits Virginia wants to leave until they get a taste of our famous ham. No cocktail party in the state would be without some version of a country ham biscuit — even our local gas station sells them. We serve this versatile, miniature rendition as part of a light lunch, with tea in the afternoon, or with drinks before dinner.

Makes about 48 biscuits

Pepper Jelly

I cup rice wine vinegar

¾ cup white wine vinegar

I jalapeño pepper, seeded and finely diced

½ green bell pepper, finely diced

½ red bell pepper, finely diced

½ yellow bell pepper, finely diced

5 cups sugar

6 ounces (2 packets) liquid pectin (sold with canning supplies)

Mascarpone Pepper Jelly

8 ounces mascarpone cheese, softened

¼ cup pepper jelly

Salt to taste

Chive Biscuits

3 cups all-purpose flour

I tablespoon salt

4 teaspoons baking powder

I tablespoon plus I teaspoon sugar

3 tablespoons finely chopped chives

1½ cups heavy cream

To Assemble and Serve

10 slices Virginia country ham, cut into small (roughly quarter-size) pieces

I small bunch frisée

For the Pepper Jelly

1. In a 4-quart stainless steel saucepan, bring the vinegars to a boil. Stir in the peppers and sugar, and simmer until the sugar has completely dissolved. Stir in the pectin.

2. Remove from heat, pour into a large heat-proof container, and cool to room temperature.

3. Refrigerate the jelly, stirring from time to time to keep the peppers evenly distributed throughout, until set. Store in the refrigerator until needed.

For the Mascarpone Pepper Jelly

In an electric mixer fitted with a paddle attachment, combine the mascarpone cheese and pepper jelly on low speed until well mixed. Season with salt.

For the Chive Biscuits

1. Preheat the oven to 350 degrees.

2. Line two baking sheets with parchment paper.

3. In a mixing bowl, combine the flour, salt, baking powder, and sugar. Add the chives.

4. Make a well in the center of the dry ingredients; add the heavy cream and stir with a wooden spoon.

5. Turn the dough out onto a lightly floured board and gently knead until it forms a ball. Roll the dough out to a thickness of ¼ inch. Using a biscuit or cookie cutter, cut out 1½-inch rounds and place them on the baking sheets.

6. Bake for 5 minutes, rotate the baking sheets, and bake for 5 minutes more, or until biscuits are barely golden. Remove the biscuits with a spatula and cool on a wire rack. Allow them to cool completely before splitting in half.

To Assemble and Serve

1. Cut the chive biscuits in half and lay them out on a board.

2. Spoon a little of the mascarpone pepper jelly on each half.

3. Place a few slices of country ham and a few leaves of frisée on each bottom half and then add the top half of the biscuit.

Barbecued Rabbit Turnovers

Like the British pasty, these miniature savory turnovers can be stuffed with a variety of fillings. Barbecued chicken is an especially good substitute if rabbit is unavailable.

These flaky crescent pastries have been a long-standing favorite of our guests. They can be fully made up, kept in the refrigerator, and baked just before serving. At the restaurant, we use the scraps from our croissant dough or puff pastry for these, but Basic Pie Dough will suffice.

For the Barbecue Sauce

In a food processor, puree all the ingredients and set aside. The sauce may be made several days in advance and stored in the refrigerator.

For the Barbecued Rabbit Filling

1. Season the rabbit meat with salt and cayenne pepper.
2. Heat the oil in a deep pot over high heat. Add the rabbit and sear the meat on all sides.
3. Add the apple cider, salt, and cayenne pepper, and cook for 1 minute.
4. Add the barbecue sauce and bring to a simmer. Cover and cook over low heat until the meat is very tender, about 1 hour. Let cool.
5. Pour the mixture into the bowl of an electric mixer fitted with a paddle attachment. Mix on medium speed until the meat is shredded and the mixture is smooth.
6. Adjust the seasoning. The filling can be made in advance and stored in the refrigerator for several days.

To Make the Turnovers

1. Preheat the oven to 375 degrees. Line 2 baking sheets with parchment paper. On a floured board, roll the dough out to about ⅛ inch thick. Stamp the dough out using a 3-inch round cutter, place the pastry rounds on the baking sheets, and refrigerate for 15 minutes.
2. Remove the pastry rounds from the refrigerator and lightly brush them with the beaten egg. Place about 1 teaspoon of filling in the center of each round. Fold the dough in half and pinch the edges closed.
3. Lightly brush the top of each filled pastry with egg and sprinkle with sesame seeds. The pastries can be assembled to this point and refrigerated overnight until ready to bake and serve.
4. Bake the pastries for 12 to 15 minutes, or until they are golden brown. Let cool for a minute or two and serve.

Makes about 40 turnovers

Barbecue Sauce

1 cup ketchup

1 medium-size Vidalia onion, quartered

½ cup white wine vinegar

¼ cup Worcestershire sauce

1 teaspoon Tabasco

2 teaspoons dry mustard

½ cup firmly packed brown sugar

Barbecued Rabbit Filling

1 three-pound rabbit, deboned
   (1 pound rabbit meat, cut into
   2-inch pieces)

1 tablespoon vegetable oil

½ cup apple cider

Salt and cayenne pepper to taste

1 recipe barbecue sauce

Turnovers

1 recipe Basic Pie Dough (see page
   200; croissant dough or puff pastry
   may be substituted)

1 egg, beaten

1 recipe barbecued rabbit filling

Sesame seeds (for garnish)

Phyllo Straws

These fragile, slender, savory pastries are addictive and are a perfect cocktail accompaniment. They can be assembled several days in advance, refrigerated, and baked before serving.

෨

1. Preheat the oven to 375 degrees.

2. On a cutting board, lay out one sheet of phyllo dough, brush with clarified butter, and sprinkle evenly with Parmesan cheese. (Keep the remaining phyllo covered with a moistened tea towel.)

3. Place the other sheet of phyllo on top of the cheese and brush it with the remaining clarified butter.

4. Using a sharp knife, cut the buttered phyllo sheets lengthwise into thirds. (You will have three long strips, each about 3 inches wide and 18 inches long.) Next, cut these strips crosswise into 1½-inch rectangles.

5. Wrap each rectangle lengthwise around a pencil or a wooden skewer. Remove the pencil or skewer and place the rolled phyllo straws on a baking sheet. Continue this process until all of the phyllo has been rolled.

6. Refrigerate the phyllo straws on the baking sheet for at least 10 minutes, or until they are firm.

7. Bake about 9 minutes, or until golden brown.

8. Remove from the oven and, using a spatula, slip the straws onto paper towels to cool. The straws may be kept in a sealed tin for several days.

Makes 24 crisps

2 sheets prepared phyllo dough,
 12 x 18 inches each

6 tablespoons clarified butter

2½ tablespoons finely grated
 Parmesan cheese

Sesame-Crusted Breadsticks

These crisp, chewy breadsticks were originally developed as a means of using the scraps of our leftover pizza dough, but soon they became so popular that we began making the dough just for them. They may be rolled in any variety of herbs or seeds. Black and white sesame seeds add additional crunch and good color contrast. We use these sticks as a garnish for the sorrel jelly on page 75.

෨

1. Preheat the oven to 350 degrees.

2. On a lightly floured board, roll the dough to about ¼ inch thick. Using a sharp knife, cut the dough into long thin strips, about 8 x ¼ inches. With your fingertips, roll each strip into ropelike sticks, about 12 inches long.

3. Lay the breadsticks on a cookie sheet lined with parchment paper. Spray them with water and sprinkle with salt and black and white sesame seeds.

4. Bake for about 10 to 15 minutes, or until the breadsticks are just barely golden on the edges.

Makes about 40 breadsticks

1 recipe Pizza Dough (see page 216)

Salt

Black sesame seeds (for garnish)

White sesame seeds (for garnish)

Bar Nuts

Here is a simple way to transform an ordinary bowl of nuts into something your guests will find tantalizing. The nuts are sautéed with aromatic spices and combined with cubed, dried pineapple. They can be made in large batches well in advance and make a wonderful gift.

෨

Makes 5 cups

4 tablespoons butter

½ teaspoon cayenne pepper

2 teaspoons Cajun seasoning

2 teaspoons ground cumin

3 tablespoons sugar

⅓ pound whole pecans

⅓ pound whole almonds

⅓ pound whole cashews

3 dried pineapple rings, cut into 1-inch pieces

Salt and sugar to taste

1. In a large skillet over medium-high heat, melt the butter. Add the cayenne, Cajun seasoning, cumin, and sugar and stir until the butter begins to foam.
2. Immediately add the pecans, almonds, and cashews, stirring or tossing constantly for about 3 minutes, or until the nuts are well toasted and lightly colored.
3. Pour the nuts onto a wire rack placed over a baking sheet. Let cool to room temperature.
4. Transfer the nuts to a mixing bowl and toss them with the dried pineapple pieces. Season to taste with salt and sugar.
5. Store in an airtight container until ready to serve.

Green Bean Tempura with Asian Dipping Sauce

These beans have become our guests' favorite finger food. We use the long, thin French green beans and present them in a silver cup lined with a parchment-paper cone. The fragrant dipping sauce is served on the side. As with any good tempura, these beans must be served immediately after frying and should be cooked in small batches.

෨

Serves 4

2 quarts vegetable or peanut oil (for deep-frying)

½ pound French green beans

1 recipe Tempura Batter (see page 220)

Salt to taste

1 recipe Clear Fish Sauce with Lime and Cilantro (see page 212)

1. In a deep fryer or heavy pot, heat the oil to 350 degrees.
2. Using a knife, cut off the tips of the green beans.
3. Dip each green bean into the Tempura Batter and shake off any excess. Carefully drop each bean into the hot oil and fry for about 1½ minutes, turning the beans with a slotted spoon until they are just golden and crisp.
4. Remove the beans from the fryer and drain them on paper towels. Season with salt and serve immediately, with the Clear Fish Sauce with Lime and Cilantro on the side.

Wild Mushroom Pizza

In the spring, our region is famous for the cone-shaped, earthy wild morel mushrooms, which our neighbors hunt in the surrounding woods. Instead of using a tomato sauce, we cover the pizza dough with a thin layer of caramelized shallots. This refined version of a thin-crust pizza is one of our favorite ways of featuring wild mushrooms. When fresh black truffles are available, we substitute them in place of the morels.

The pizzas can be fully assembled, kept in the refrigerator, and baked just before serving. They make a great first course or can be cut into very thin slices and served as cocktail-party finger food.

To achieve a crackling-crisp crust, we bake the pizzas on a hot stone slab laid on the oven floor (or on the lowest rack). These pizza stones can be purchased in many cookware and department stores.

℘

Makes 6 individual pizzas

Caramelized Shallots

4 tablespoons unsalted butter

2 cups peeled, sliced shallots

Salt and freshly ground black pepper
    to taste

Pizza

3 tablespoons olive oil

3 cups fresh morel mushrooms, halved

½ teaspoon finely chopped garlic

1 teaspoon finely chopped shallots

Salt and freshly ground black pepper
    to taste

1 recipe Pizza Dough (see page 216)

Cornmeal (to dust baking sheet)

1 recipe caramelized shallots

1¼ cups freshly grated Parmesan
    cheese (about 3 ounces)

⅔ cup grated Fontina cheese
    (about 3 ounces)

3 spears asparagus, cut on the bias into
    thin slices, blanched and refreshed

2 very thin slices of well-trimmed
    country ham, cut into thin strips

For the Caramelized Shallots

1. In a heavy-bottomed saucepan, melt the butter over medium heat and add the sliced shallots. Reduce the heat to low and cook, stirring occasionally, for 30 minutes, or until golden brown.

2. Season with salt and pepper and cool to room temperature.

For the Pizza

1. Place a pizza stone in the oven and preheat to 450 degrees.

2. In a large skillet, heat 2 tablespoons of the olive oil over high heat. Add the morel mushrooms and sauté for 2 minutes. Add the garlic and shallots and sauté for 1 minute more. Remove from heat, season with salt and pepper, and set aside.

3. On a floured board, roll out the pizza dough to about ⅛ inch thick. Lay a bowl about 5 inches in diameter upside down on the dough and, using the rim as a pattern, cut out six circles with a sharp paring knife. Dust a cookie sheet with cornmeal and place the pizza rounds on top of it.

4. Spread a thin layer of caramelized shallots onto each pizza round, leaving a ½-inch border of dough exposed around the edges.

5. Lightly sprinkle a layer of Parmesan over the caramelized shallots, reserving a few tablespoons of cheese for finishing the pizzas.

6. Arrange the morel mushrooms on top of the caramelized shallots and sprinkle with Fontina cheese.

7. Using a spatula, carefully slide the pizzas onto the hot stone and bake until the crust is crisp and golden brown.

8. Sprinkle the asparagus slices onto the pizzas and drizzle them with the remaining tablespoon of olive oil. Return the pizzas to the oven and cook for 1 more minute.

9. Remove the pizzas from the oven and sprinkle with country ham and the remaining Parmesan cheese.

Lacy Parmesan Wafers

These delicate, crisp wafers are incredibly simple to make and perfect to nibble with a glass of champagne. They can be made in advance, kept in a sealed tin, and offered as a gift during the holidays. Our guests love them.

৪৩

Makes 24 wafers

2 cups (about 8 ounces) freshly grated
  Parmesan cheese

1. Preheat the oven to 350 degrees.

2. On a nonstick cookie sheet or one lined with a Silpat sheet, place 2 teaspoons of cheese in a little mound. Using the back of a teaspoon, spread the mound out into a circle about 2½ inches in diameter. Repeat, keeping about 1 inch between each circle.

3. Bake for 4 to 5 minutes, just until the wafers turn crisp and golden brown. Remove from the oven. Allow them to cool on the Silpat. Using a spatula, remove the wafers and store in a tightly sealed tin at room temperature.

Note: This recipe can be used to make edible Parmesan "baskets" or containers. Simply slip the wafers, while still warm, off the cookie sheet and drape them over the back of a small bowl. Cool and serve.

Brittle Bread Crackers

This delicious flatbread is a perfect accompaniment to a cheese course. The basic dough can be sprinkled with sesame, poppy, or caraway seeds before baking. The crackers can be kept for several days in an airtight tin.

৪৩

Makes about 72 crackers

2¾ cups all-purpose flour

¼ cup sugar

½ teaspoon salt

½ teaspoon baking soda

¼ pound (1 stick) cold unsalted butter,
  cut into ½-inch pieces

½ pound mascarpone cheese

1 egg, beaten

Coarse salt

Garnishes

Sesame seeds

Poppy seeds

Caraway seeds

1. Combine the flour, sugar, salt, and baking soda in a food processor.

2. Add the butter and process until the mixture resembles coarse cornmeal. Add the mascarpone and process until it is just combined.

3. Wrap the dough tightly in plastic wrap, and refrigerate for at least 10 minutes.

4. When you are ready to make the crackers, preheat the oven to 350 degrees.

5. Roll out the dough on a lightly floured surface until it is paper thin and prick it several times with a fork. Using a pastry brush, lightly coat the dough with the beaten egg and sprinkle with coarse salt.

6. With a sharp knife or pizza cutter, cut the dough into random cracker shapes. Sprinkle some of the crackers with sesame, poppy, or caraway seeds.

7. Place the crackers on a baking sheet in a single layer and bake for about 8 to 10 minutes, or until golden and crisp.

Rosemary and Roasted Garlic Cornbread Madeleines

Using fluted madeleine cookie molds to bake this rosemary-scented corn-bread makes for a refined rendition of an American pioneer food. If you don't have madeleine molds, substitute miniature muffin tins.

80

1. Preheat the oven to 350 degrees. Spray several madeleine molds with non-stick cooking spray.
2. In the bowl of an electric mixer fitted with a paddle attachment, cream the butter and sugar together until light and fluffy. Add the egg, buttermilk, and Roasted Garlic and beat to combine.
3. In a separate mixing bowl, combine the cornmeal, flour, baking powder, baking soda, salt, and rosemary.
4. With the mixer on low speed, slowly add the flour mixture and mix until the batter is smooth.
5. Using a teaspoon, fill the madeleine molds half full with batter. Bake for 5 minutes. Remove the madeleines from the molds and cool on a wire rack.

Makes 48 miniature madeleines

Nonstick cooking spray

6 tablespoons unsalted butter (¾ stick), softened

½ cup sugar

1 egg

1 cup buttermilk

½ tablespoon Roasted Garlic (see page 217)

1 cup plus 2 tablespoons yellow cornmeal

1¼ cups flour

½ teaspoon baking powder

⅛ teaspoon baking soda

½ teaspoon salt

1 tablespoon finely chopped rosemary

Lilliputian Bacon, Lettuce, and Tomato Sandwiches

A wise man once told me that America's equivalent to Chinese Peking duck is the bacon, lettuce, and tomato sandwich. That statement forever deepened my appreciation of a lunchtime standby we so easily take for granted. When all of the ingredients are perfect, the combination of taste and texture in a good BLT is hard to beat. The bacon must be wonderfully flavorful and served warm.

This elegant miniaturization of an American classic makes a charming summertime canapé.

Makes 12 canapés

12 one-inch squares of thinly sliced
   white bread, toasted

2 tablespoons good-quality
   mayonnaise, preferably homemade

½ cup frisée

4 plum tomatoes or 6 cherry
   tomatoes, sliced

Salt and freshly ground black pepper
   to taste

3 strips cooked bacon, cut into
   1-inch pieces

Baby chervil leaves

1. Lay the toast squares on a board. Place a small dollop of mayonnaise on each.

2. Place a small sprig of frisée on the mayonnaise, follow with a slice of tomato, sprinkle with salt and pepper, and finish with a piece of warm bacon.

3. Garnish with a chervil leaf.

Dilled Deviled Quail Eggs

These miniature deviled quail eggs are right out of Alice's Adventures in Wonderland *and will add a welcome note of whimsy to your table. The hard-boiled yolks are flavored and tinted with a piquant mustard-dill sauce rather than mayonnaise. Naturally, the same method can be used for regular-size eggs. The mustard-dill sauce also makes a delicious accompaniment for smoked salmon or gravlax.*

For the Mustard-Dill Sauce

1. Place the dill and sugar in a food processor and pulse until coarsely chopped. Scrape down the sides of the bowl with a rubber spatula and pulse again.

2. Add the Dijon mustard, dry mustard, white wine vinegar, vegetable oil, and lemon juice and blend thoroughly. Season to taste with salt and pepper.

3. Store in the refrigerator until ready to use.

For the Deviled Quail Eggs

1. Bring a small pot of salted water to a boil over high heat. Gently add the eggs, reduce the heat, and simmer. Cook for 5 minutes. Using a slotted spoon, remove the eggs from the boiling water and immediately place them in a bowl of ice water. Allow them to chill completely.

2. Remove the eggshells, being careful not to damage the eggs. Using a sharp paring knife, split each quail egg in half lengthwise. Carefully remove the yolks and place them in a small mixing bowl.

3. Using a fork, combine the cooked egg yolks, mustard-dill sauce, salt, and pepper.

4. Using a small spoon or pastry tip, fill the egg whites with the yolk mixture. Garnish with minced chives. Serve on a bed of fresh dill sprigs.

Makes 24 deviled eggs

Mustard-Dill Sauce

Makes 2 cups

⅔ cup dill sprigs, large stems removed

½ cup sugar

¾ cup Dijon mustard

2 teaspoons dry mustard

⅓ cup white wine vinegar

¾ cup vegetable oil

2 tablespoons fresh lemon juice

Salt and freshly ground black pepper to taste

Deviled Quail Eggs

12 fresh quail eggs (available at gourmet grocery stores)

1 tablespoon mustard-dill sauce

Salt and freshly ground black pepper to taste

½ cup minced fresh chives

Fresh dill sprigs for garnish

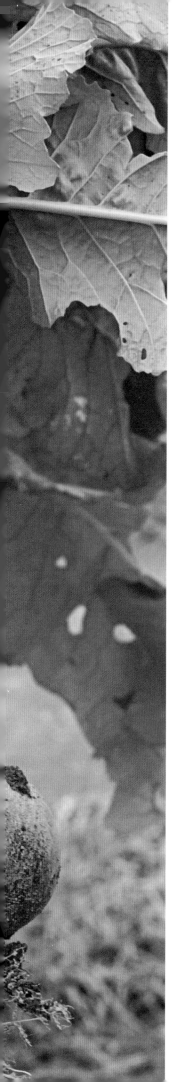

Soups

৪৩

Watermelon-Tequila Soup

On a hot summer day when watermelons are in season, this cold, sassy soup is a refreshing surprise and can be made in just a few minutes.

&

Makes about 2½ quarts
(6 to 8 servings)

1 small watermelon, about 6 pounds
1 cup heavy cream
Pinch of sugar, if needed
1 bunch fresh cilantro
⅓ cup tequila

1. Split the watermelon in half and scoop out the pulp with a large spoon. Discard the rind.

2. Puree the watermelon in a food processor. (Don't worry about the seeds. They will get strained out later.)

3. Strain the pureed watermelon through a fine mesh sieve.

4. Whisk in the cream and adjust the sweetness with sugar, if needed.

5. Tie the cilantro together with kitchen string. Drop it into the soup and bruise the leaves with a wooden spoon to release their flavor. Refrigerate the soup for several hours or overnight with the cilantro in it.

6. Just before serving, remove the cilantro and add the tequila.

Chilled Plum Soup

When plums are plentiful, a demitasse of this cold fruit soup is an elegant and unusual way to begin a summer dinner.

&

1. In a 4-quart saucepan, combine the plums, apple cider, and brown sugar.
2. Place the lemon, orange, cinnamon stick, ginger root, and clove in the center of the cheesecloth square, draw up the corners to form a little bundle, and tie it closed with the string, making a sachet. Add the sachet to the saucepan.
3. Bring the mixture to a boil over high heat, reduce the heat, and simmer for 20 minutes.
4. Carefully remove the sachet from the liquid and discard.
5. Puree the soup in a food processor or blender and strain through a fine mesh sieve.
6. Add the heavy cream and Simple Syrup.
7. Refrigerate the soup for several hours or overnight.
8. Just before serving, whisk the optional crème fraîche in a small bowl until it is runny. Ladle the soup into demitasse cups and finish each one with a swirl of crème fraîche.

Makes about 2½ quarts
(6 to 8 servings)

2½ pounds black or red plums, pitted, skins on

4½ cups apple cider

½ cup brown sugar

4 thin slices of lemon

4 thin slices of orange

1 three-inch cinnamon stick

1 tablespoon peeled, chopped fresh ginger root

1 clove

1 piece cheesecloth (10 inches x 10 inches)

1 twelve-inch length of kitchen string

2 cups heavy cream

1 cup Simple Syrup (see page 218)

⅓ cup crème fraîche (optional)

Watercress Soup

This is a simple but luxurious soup that can be quickly assembled. Searing the watercress briefly in hot oil and quickly pureeing it into the soup base helps retain a desirable, vibrant green color. Straining the soup gives it an airy and elegant texture. If you don't have chicken stock or want to make a vegetarian soup, water can be substituted with surprisingly good results.

Makes about 2 quarts
(6 to 8 servings)

5 tablespoons unsalted butter

2 medium yellow onions, diced

1 medium Idaho potato, peeled
and diced

6 cups chicken stock

4 tablespoons vegetable oil

4 bunches watercress, large stems
removed

½ cup heavy cream

Salt, freshly ground white pepper,
and sugar to taste

2 tablespoons watercress leaves

2 strips bacon, diced, fried until crisp,
and drained

1. In a 4-quart saucepan, melt 3 tablespoons of the unsalted butter over medium heat. Add the onions and cook until tender but not browned.

2. Add the potato and continue cooking for 3 minutes.

3. Add the stock and bring to a boil. Lower the heat and simmer until the potatoes are soft, about 10 to 15 minutes. Remove from heat.

4. In a 10-inch sauté pan, heat 1 tablespoon of oil until almost smoking. Add a handful of watercress to the pan, tossing and turning rapidly with tongs. After a few seconds, when the watercress is just wilted and has turned a vibrant green color, add it to the soup. Repeat this process with the remaining watercress.

5. Puree the soup in a blender or food processor and, if desired, strain.

6. Just before serving, return the soup to the stove over medium heat, and whisk in the cream and the remaining 2 tablespoons of butter. Season with salt, white pepper, and sugar.

7. Serve the soup in individual bowls garnished with watercress leaves and crispy bacon.

Cream of Mussel Soup

This elegant mussel soup, perfumed with the intriguing flavors of saffron, curry, orange zest, and Pernod (an anise-flavored French aperitif), is reminiscent of a fragrant bouillabaisse but much easier to make. Straining the soup gives it a velvety texture, while the addition of a little cream softens and blends all of the striking flavors.

To Cook the Mussels

1. Throw away any mussels that have broken shells or that are not tightly closed.

2. In a saucepan large enough to hold all of the mussels after they open, bring the wine, parsley, thyme, bay leaf, and shallots to a boil. Add the mussels; cover and steam for about 3 minutes, or until the mussels open.

3. Transfer the mussels to a bowl and reserve the liquid. Remove the mussels from their shells. Strain the mussel cooking liquid and set aside.

To Make the Soup

1. In a soup pot, melt the butter over medium heat. Add the fennel seeds and cook for 1 minute. Add the onions and curry powder and cook for about 5 minutes, or until the onions are soft and translucent.

2. Add the white wine, tomato or V8 juice, tomatoes, thyme, bay leaf, and saffron and simmer, stirring occasionally, for 30 minutes.

3. Puree the soup in batches in a blender and return it to the soup pot. Add the cooked, shelled mussels and their cooking liquid to the puree and simmer for 10 minutes. Strain the soup through a fine mesh sieve, pressing lightly on the mussels to extract all their juices. (The mussels may be discarded or saved for another use.) Return the soup to the pot.

4. Add the heavy cream and Pernod and simmer for 5 minutes. Add the orange peel and simmer for another 5 minutes. Remove the orange peel with a slotted spoon. Season the soup with salt and cayenne pepper.

5. If the soup seems too thick, it can be thinned with a little tomato or V8 juice.

Makes about 2 quarts
(6 to 8 servings)

Mussels

1 pound mussels

⅓ cup dry white wine

2 sprigs fresh parsley stems

1 sprig fresh thyme

½ bay leaf

1 teaspoon chopped shallots

Soup

1 tablespoon butter

½ teaspoon fennel seeds

3 cups sliced onion

1 teaspoon curry powder

⅓ cup dry white wine

⅓ cup tomato or V8 juice

1¾ cups canned chopped tomatoes

1 sprig fresh thyme

½ bay leaf

6 saffron "threads"

Cooked, shelled mussels and their cooking liquid (from previous procedure)

1½ cups heavy cream

3 tablespoons Pernod

1 strip orange peel

Salt and cayenne pepper to taste

Tomato or V8 juice for thinning, if needed

Puree of Parsnip Soup

I am always surprised by the number of people who have never tasted a parsnip. When they do, they're always intrigued by the old-fashioned, subtly sweet, rich flavor of the "forgotten" vegetable. This earthy but elegant soup will make a soul-satisfying addition to any fall or winter menu.

ร

1. In a large saucepan over medium-high heat, melt the butter. Add the parsnips, carrot, onion, and celery with a pinch of salt and cook, stirring occasionally, until the onions are translucent.
2. Add the chicken or Vegetable Stock and bay leaf and bring to a boil. Simmer for 20 to 25 minutes, or until all of the vegetables are cooked through and tender.
3. Puree the vegetables in a blender or food processor. Strain through a fine mesh sieve into the same pot you used to cook the vegetables. Add the heavy cream, salt, pepper, and nutmeg. Return the pan to the stove, bring the soup to a simmer, and serve.

Makes about 2 quarts
(6 to 8 servings)

2 tablespoons butter

1½ pounds parsnips, peeled and roughly chopped

1 carrot, peeled and roughly chopped

½ onion, roughly chopped

1 stalk celery, roughly chopped

1½ quarts chicken or Vegetable Stock (see page 221)

1 bay leaf

2 cups heavy cream

Salt and freshly ground white pepper to taste

Freshly grated nutmeg to taste

Apple-Rutabaga Soup

I only recently rediscovered rutabagas and am so happy I did. They were something my mother used to prepare when we were kids — usually as a puree — and even though I thought they tasted a little weird, their gorgeous golden color always made me want another mouthful.

This soup looks and tastes like liquid autumn. All year long we look forward to serving it again in the fall. It's incredibly simple to put together and can be made well in advance and frozen. The elusive secret ingredient is a bit of maple syrup, which enhances the natural sweetness of the rutabaga.

Water or vegetable stock may be successfully substituted for the chicken stock if you wish to make this soup vegetarian, or if you don't want to bother making chicken stock.

ଅ

Makes about 2 quarts
(6 to 8 servings)

¼ pound (1 stick) butter

1 cup roughly chopped onion

1 cup peeled, cored, and roughly chopped Granny Smith apple

1 cup peeled and roughly chopped rutabaga

1 cup peeled, seeded, and roughly chopped butternut squash

1 cup peeled and roughly chopped carrots

1 cup peeled and roughly chopped sweet potato

1 quart good chicken stock

2 cups heavy cream

¼ cup maple syrup

Salt and cayenne pepper to taste

1. In a large saucepan over medium-high heat, melt the butter. Add the onion, apple, rutabaga, squash, carrots, and sweet potato and cook, stirring occasionally, until the onions are translucent.

2. Add the chicken stock and bring to a boil. Simmer for 20 to 25 minutes or until all of the vegetables are cooked through and tender.

3. Puree the vegetables in a blender or food processor. Strain through a fine mesh sieve into the same pot you used to cook the vegetables. Add the cream, maple syrup, salt, and cayenne pepper.

4. Return the pot to the stove, bring the soup to a simmer, and serve.

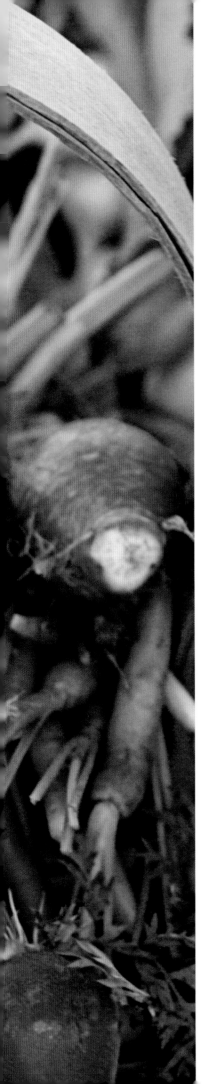

Cold First Courses

&)

Beet Carpaccio

This is a way to turn a humble, inexpensive root vegetable into a stylish first course. At first glance, the thinly sliced red beets look almost like the classic beef carpaccio, named for the artist whose roseate sunsets resemble the colors of raw beef and thus inspired the name.

Roasting the beets brings out their natural sweetness and intensifies their flavor. The beets can be roasted, sliced, preplated, and kept in the refrigerator. They should be garnished and dressed just before serving. The extravagant garnishes of caviar and vodka aspic are completely optional.

ℰℂ

For the Beets

1. Preheat the oven to 350 degrees.
2. Rinse the beets in cold water. In a baking dish large enough to hold the beets in a single layer, toss the beets with the olive oil, vinegar, rosemary, and thyme.
3. Cover the dish with foil and roast the beets for 40 to 50 minutes, or until the baby yellow beets are tender when pierced with the sharp point of a paring knife. Remove the baby yellow beets and continue to roast the red beets for an additional 25 minutes, or until tender.

To Make the Orange Vinaigrette

Whisk all the ingredients together in a large stainless steel bowl. Transfer to a jar with a tight-fitting lid. The vinaigrette can be made in advance and stored in the refrigerator. Shake well or whisk thoroughly before serving.

For the Vodka Aspic (optional)

1. In a small saucepan, bring the vodka to a boil over medium heat, being careful not to ignite it.
2. Whisk in the pectin and bring the mixture back to a boil. Reduce the heat and simmer for 1 minute.
3. Pour the mixture into a pie pan or small, shallow container so that the liquid is about ½ inch deep.
4. Refrigerate the mixture overnight, or until it has jelled completely. Cut the aspic into cubes.

To Serve

1. When the beets are cool enough to handle, peel them with a small paring knife. Cut the baby yellow beets into wedges.
2. Using a mandoline (an adjustable slicer with a sharp blade), slice the red beets ⅛ inch thick and arrange them in overlapping concentric circles on each plate.
3. Place an oval dollop of crème fraîche on the beets and a smaller dollop of caviar (if desired) on top of the crème fraîche.
4. Garnish each plate with a few wedges of yellow beets, orange zest, chervil or mint sprigs, and (if desired) vodka aspic. Splash the orange vinaigrette over the beets.

Serves 4

Beets

8 medium beets, unpeeled

4 baby yellow beets, unpeeled

⅔ cup olive oil

⅓ cup balsamic vinegar

4 sprigs rosemary

6 sprigs thyme

Orange Vinaigrette

1½ cups fresh orange juice

3 tablespoons chopped tarragon

½ cup white wine vinegar

¼ cup walnut oil

½ cup olive oil

1 tablespoon minced shallots

1 teaspoon minced garlic

Salt and freshly ground black pepper to taste

Vodka Aspic (optional)

1 cup citron-flavored vodka

¼ cup pectin

Garnishes

¼ cup crème fraîche

1 ounce osetra caviar (optional)

Orange zest

Chervil or mint sprigs

Mélange of Jumbo Lump Crab, Mango, and Avocado in a Tropical Fruit Puree

When sweet, succulent jumbo lump crabmeat comes into season, this dish is an incredibly simple, light, and refreshing first course, which requires no cooking. It can also be served as a main course for a summer luncheon.

Serves 4

Tropical Fruit Puree

1 cup roughly chopped cantaloupe

½ cup roughly chopped fresh pineapple

½ bunch fresh cilantro

1 12-inch length of kitchen string

2 teaspoons fresh lime juice

Pinch of sugar, to taste

Crab Salad

1 pound jumbo lump crabmeat

1½ tablespoons minced jalapeño pepper, ribs and seeds removed

2 tablespoons lemon juice

1½ tablespoons nuoc mam (fermented fish sauce, available in Asian markets as Vietnamese Nuoc Mam)

2 tablespoons roughly chopped fresh cilantro

½ avocado, pit removed

¼ cup fresh diced mango

For the Tropical Fruit Puree

1. Puree the cantaloupe and pineapple in a food processor. Transfer the puree to a mixing bowl.

2. Tie the cilantro together with kitchen string and add it to the fruit puree. Stir in the lime juice.

3. Cover and refrigerate for at least half an hour or overnight. Remove the cilantro and add a pinch of sugar to taste. The tropical fruit puree can be made in advance and stored overnight in the refrigerator until ready to serve.

To Make the Crab Salad

1. Pick through the crabmeat carefully to be sure that all of the shells and cartilage are removed.

2. With a rubber spatula, gently fold the crabmeat, jalapeño, lemon juice, nuoc mam, and cilantro together in a mixing bowl.

3. Place a 2½-inch round ring mold or cookie cutter on 1 of 4 chilled plates. With a teaspoon, scoop 2 tablespoons of avocado from the shell, place it inside the mold, and pack it down lightly with the back of a spoon.

4. Place 1 tablespoon of diced mango on top of the avocado and press it down gently.

5. Fill the rest of the mold with the crab mixture. Smooth off the top with the flat side of a knife. Carefully lift the mold from the mélange.

6. Repeat this process with the remaining plates.

7. Ladle the tropical fruit puree around the edges of the mélange and serve chilled.

Sorrel Jelly with Lemon Cream and Osetra Caviar

I grew up eating "wood's sorrel," which we called "sour grass." It grew wild in the garden like a weed and resembled clover. In my kitchen today, I use the cultivated variety called French sorrel, which looks like spinach. In the spring and summer months, French sorrel is often available at farmer's markets, and it is easy to grow from seed. The intensely tart, lemony flavor of this leafy green is singularly unique and has become a hallmark of our spring menus at The Inn.

This wildly refreshing, chilled first course is easier to make than a soup and far more interesting. We serve it in small square shot glasses; however, demitasse cups or martini glasses will also work. Of course, the caviar garnish may be omitted. The Sesame-Crusted Breadsticks are a pleasant crunchy accompaniment.

To Make the Sorrel Jelly

1. Puree the cream and sorrel in a blender.

2. Add the vinegar and lemon juice and season with salt and pepper.

3. Place the cold chicken stock in a small heat-proof bowl and sprinkle the gelatin over it. When the gelatin has softened, place the bowl over a small pot of simmering water until the gelatin has completely dissolved.

4. Combine the gelatin and sorrel mixtures and strain through a fine mesh sieve. Refrigerate the sorrel mixture for 1 hour, until it is well chilled but not set.

5. Pour about ¼ cup of the mixture into each of 8 shot glasses, demitasse cups, or martini glasses. Chill in the refrigerator overnight, or until set.

To Make the Lemon Cream

In a large mixing bowl, combine the crème fraîche, heavy cream, and lemon juice with a whisk. Season with salt, pepper, and sugar.

To Serve and Garnish

1. Pour 1 tablespoon of lemon cream on top of the sorrel jelly in each glass.

2. If desired, place a small oval of caviar on top of the lemon cream.

3. Garnish the glasses with the 8 small sorrel leaves and serve each glass of sorrel jelly, accompanied by a breadstick and a demitasse spoon, on its own small plate.

Serves 8

Sorrel Jelly

1 cup heavy cream

1½ cups loosely packed sorrel leaves, washed, stems removed

½ cup red wine vinegar

2 tablespoons lemon juice

Salt and white pepper to taste

1 cup cold chicken stock

1½ teaspoons powdered gelatin

Lemon Cream

½ cup crème fraîche

½ cup heavy cream

2 tablespoons lemon juice

Salt, freshly ground white pepper, and sugar to taste

Garnishes

1 ounce osetra caviar, optional

8 small sorrel leaves

8 Sesame-Crusted Breadsticks (see page 41)

Chilled Maine Lobster with Lemon-Caviar Vinaigrette

When the occasion calls for something extravagant, there is nothing more luxurious than cold lobster and caviar. One ounce of caviar goes a long way in flavoring the vinaigrette sauce and will be enough to serve four in this recipe. There is no substitute for good-quality, fresh caviar, so if you can't get it, it's best to simply omit it. In the restaurant, we use the sweeter Meyer lemons when they are available, but regular lemons will suffice.

After years of experimenting with different ways of cooking lobster, we have concluded that the following method of steaming the claws and pan roasting the tails yields maximum flavor and tenderness, and solves the usual problem of the tails overcooking before the claws are done.

This is one of our most popular first courses — especially in warm weather — but it also makes an ideal main course for an elegant summer lunch or wedding. All of the components can be prepared the night before and assembled just before serving.

ঈ

Serves 4

Meyer Lemon Vinaigrette

¼ cup lemon juice, preferably from Meyer lemons

1 egg yolk

3 tablespoons crème fraîche

2 tablespoons orange juice

Salt to taste

½ cup extra virgin olive oil

1 cup vegetable oil

1 ounce osetra caviar (optional)

Lobster

2 live lobsters, about 1½ pounds each

2 tablespoons vegetable oil

¼ cup white wine

1 tablespoon lemon juice, preferably from Meyer lemons

3 tablespoons extra virgin olive oil

For the Meyer Lemon Vinaigrette

1. In a food processor, combine the lemon juice, egg yolk, crème fraîche, orange juice, and salt.

2. With the food processor running, slowly add the oils in a thin stream.

3. Cover and refrigerate until ready to use.

4. Just before serving, fold in ½ ounce of the caviar (if desired), reserving the remaining caviar for garnish.

To Cook the Lobster Claws

1. Hold the lobsters with a kitchen towel and carefully pull off the claws and tails. (Discard the bodies or keep them to flavor a lobster stock or soup.)

2. In a kettle or steamer, bring 2 inches of salted water to a rolling boil. Add the lobster claws, cover, and cook for 8 minutes.

3. Remove the claws from the steamer and plunge them into ice water to stop the cooking. Remove the claws from the ice water.

4. Using a mallet, carefully crack the claws and remove the meat in whole pieces. Refrigerate the meat until ready to use.

To Cook the Lobster Tails

1. Using a sharp knife, cut through the center of the shells, dividing the raw tails in half lengthwise. Leave the meat in the shells.

2. In a heavy-bottomed saucepan, heat the vegetable oil over high heat until almost smoking. Carefully add the split lobster tails in their shells, cover, and cook for 3 minutes. (Caution: The hot oil may splatter when the tails are added to the pan.)

3. Add the white wine, cover, and cook for 1 minute more.

4. Transfer the lobster tails to a mixing bowl and toss them with the lemon

juice and extra virgin olive oil. Cool to room temperature and remove the tail meat from the shells. Refrigerate until ready to use.

To Serve and Garnish

1. Toss a small bouquet of mixed greens with a few tablespoons of Meyer lemon vinaigrette and place in the center of each plate. Sprinkle a few Pickled Red Onions on top. Fan a few slices of avocado beside the greens.

2. Slice each of the lobster tail halves crosswise into thirds and rest them on the greens in an arc opposite the avocado. Lay a lobster claw next to the tail meat.

3. Place an oval dollop of crème fraîche on each plate and place a smaller dollop of the remaining caviar on top.

4. Garnish each plate with a few lemon sections.

5. Spoon the remaining Meyer lemon vinaigrette over the lobster tails and drizzle it around the plate.

Garnishes

1 cup loosely packed baby greens, frisée, or watercress

½ cup Meyer lemon vinaigrette

1 recipe Pickled Red Onions (optional, see page 215)

1 ripe avocado

2 tablespoons crème fraîche

Caviar (reserved from Meyer lemon vinaigrette)

1 lemon, rind and pith removed, sectioned

Fire and Ice: Seared Peppered Tuna with Daikon Radish and Cucumber Sorbet

In this recipe, the spicy "heat" of the seared peppered tuna (still raw in the center) is intriguingly juxtaposed with an intensely flavored, icy and refreshing Cucumber Sorbet. The tuna is mounded on a little nest of dressed vermicelli and garnished with cucumber salsa. While this dish may initially strike you as strange or unapproachable, it is neither. If you don't have time to make the Cucumber Sorbet, the tuna will still be delicious without it. Once you've tried this dish, it will become a staple in your summer entertaining repertoire.

Serves 6

Vermicelli Noodles

3 tablespoons soy sauce

1 teaspoon nuoc mam (fermented fish sauce, available in Asian markets as Vietnamese Nuoc Mam)

2 tablespoons rice wine vinegar

1 teaspoon sugar

2 teaspoons peanut oil

1 tablespoon mustard seeds

¼ cup thinly sliced red onion

2 tablespoons fresh cilantro leaves

2 ounces vermicelli rice noodles or angel hair pasta

Soy Dressing

1 cup soy sauce

¼ cup rice wine vinegar

¼ cup sugar

¾ cup finely grated fresh daikon radish (available in Asian markets or specialty produce sections)

Peppered Tuna

2 tablespoons black peppercorns

8 ounces very fresh loin of tuna

1 teaspoon vegetable oil

To Serve

Cilantro leaves (for garnish)

½ cup cucumber salsa (see Cucumber Sorbet on page 124)

1 cup Cucumber Sorbet (see page 124)

For the Vermicelli Noodles

1. In a mixing bowl, combine the soy sauce, nuoc mam, rice wine vinegar, sugar, peanut oil, mustard seeds, red onion, and cilantro leaves and set aside.

2. In a large pot, bring 2 quarts of salted water to a boil. Add the vermicelli and cook for 2 to 3 minutes, until the noodles are al dente. Drain the noodles, rinse them with cold water, and add them to the soy sauce mixture. The noodles may be made ahead of time and stored for several hours in the refrigerator until ready to serve.

For the Soy Dressing

In a small mixing bowl, combine the soy sauce, rice wine vinegar, sugar, and daikon radish. This may be made several days ahead of time and stored in the refrigerator until ready to serve.

For the Peppered Tuna

1. Place the peppercorns on a wooden cutting board and crack them coarsely with the bottom of a small heavy saucepan.

2. Press the cracked peppercorns onto both sides of the tuna.

3. In a cast-iron skillet, heat the vegetable oil over high heat.

4. Sear the tuna for 45 seconds on both sides.

5. Transfer the tuna to a cutting board and slice it into ⅛-inch-thick slices.

To Serve

1. In each of 6 serving bowls, place a few tablespoons of soy dressing.

2. Arrange a small mound of vermicelli noodles in the center of each bowl.

3. Fan 4 or 5 slices of tuna over the noodles and garnish with cilantro leaves.

4. Place 1 tablespoon of cucumber salsa and a small scoop of Cucumber Sorbet on top of the tuna.

Shavings of Country Ham with Parmesan, Pears, and Pine Nuts

This first course requires no cooking and clearly demonstrates the stunning effect a few simple ingredients of the finest quality can have when thoughtfully combined. All of the elements are intended to complement the unique flavors of a good ham and can be assembled in just a few minutes.

Our kitchen staff has nicknamed this dish "The Fluffy" because I am constantly reminding them that it should look light and airy, as if the ingredients floated from the sky down onto the plate.

Serves 6

½-pound block of Parmesan cheese

12 very thin slices of country ham (preferably Virginia), cut into wide ribbons

1 ripe pear, halved and cored (unpeeled)

1 bunch baby arugula, washed and stemmed

¼ cup toasted pine nuts

4 tablespoons extra virgin olive oil

Cracked black pepper to taste

1. Using a vegetable peeler or cheese slicer, shave the Parmesan cheese into "ribbons."

2. Intertwine a few ribbons of cheese and ham on each of 6 plates to form a small, fluffy mound.

3. Using a mandoline or sharp knife, slice the pear as thinly as possible. Add a few pear slices to each mound of cheese and ham.

4. Over each plate, toss a few leaves of baby arugula, sprinkle with pine nuts, and drizzle with extra virgin olive oil. Garnish with cracked black pepper.

Hot First Courses

80

Pistachio Prawns Stuffed with Crabmeat on Wilted Watercress

We use giant farm-raised, head-on freshwater prawns for this dish, but any big shrimp will work as well. Colorful crushed pistachio nuts are sprinkled on top of the crabmeat stuffing along with Panko flakes (Japanese bread-crumbs) to add a crunchy texture and a toasty, buttery flavor. The prawns or shrimp can be stuffed, kept in the refrigerator for several hours, and baked just before serving.

૭ઝ

Serves 6

Stuffed Prawns

½ cup shelled, ground pistachios

⅓ cup Panko flakes (Japanese breadcrumbs, sold in Asian markets)

2 tablespoons chopped fresh parsley

1 teaspoon grated lemon zest

1 tablespoon lemon juice

2 tablespoons Brown Butter (see page 212)

6 ounces jumbo lump crabmeat

6 large freshwater prawns

Nonstick cooking spray

Salt and freshly ground black pepper to taste

2 tablespoons extra virgin olive oil

Garnishes

1 recipe Wilted Watercress (see page 169)

½ cup Tomato Vinaigrette (see page 221)

¼ cup mustard-dill sauce (see Dilled Deviled Quail Eggs on page 51)

1 tablespoon extra virgin olive oil

For the Stuffed Prawns

1. Preheat the oven to 350 degrees.

2. In a small mixing bowl, combine the pistachios, Panko flakes, parsley, lemon zest, lemon juice, and Brown Butter.

3. Pick through the crabmeat carefully, removing any shell and cartilage.

4. Leaving the head intact, peel each prawn, except for the tip of the tail. Lay each prawn on its back and, using a paring knife, make an incision from just above the tip of the tail to just below the head.

5. Spray a baking sheet with nonstick spray. Place the prawns on their back on the baking sheet, flatten them out, season with salt and pepper, and stuff them with crabmeat. Cover the crabmeat with the breadcrumb mixture and sprinkle with olive oil.

6. Bake for about 12 minutes, or until the breadcrumbs are golden brown and the prawns are just cooked through.

To Serve

1. Place a small nest of Wilted Watercress in the center of each of 6 serving plates.

2. Dot the plates with pools of Tomato Vinaigrette and mustard-dill sauce.

3. Lay one prawn on top of each mound of watercress, drizzle a bit of extra virgin olive oil over the prawns, and serve.

Glazed Oysters Drunk on Champagne

Three favorite indulgences — oysters, champagne, and caviar — are combined in this dish. The oysters are poached in their shells with champagne, napped with a champagne hollandaise, given a golden glaze under the broiler, and finished with a decadent dollop of caviar. The oysters emerge barely warmed through and more seductive than ever. We serve them on a bed of rock salt or blanched seaweed.

&

Makes 24 oysters

Champagne Hollandaise Sauce

1 pound butter

3 egg yolks

¼ teaspoon cornstarch (optional)

¼ cup champagne

¼ cup cold water

2 teaspoons fresh lemon juice

Pinch each of salt, paprika, cayenne pepper, and freshly ground white pepper

Oysters

24 large fresh oysters

½ pound fresh spinach

2 tablespoons butter

Pinch each of salt and sugar

Freshly ground black pepper to taste

½ cup champagne

4 ounces caviar (optional)

For the Champagne Hollandaise Sauce

1. Melt one pound of butter and keep warm.

2. Place the egg yolks, cornstarch (optional), champagne, and cold water in the top of a double boiler or in a stainless steel bowl. Set the mixture over a pot of simmering water and whisk vigorously until the yolks begin to thicken. Continue whisking until the yolks are pale yellow and very thick, about 6 to 8 minutes. Do not overcook, or the yolks may scramble.

3. Remove the yolks from heat and slowly begin to whisk in the warm butter. Add all of the butter except for the milky residue in the bottom of the pan.

4. Whisk in the lemon juice, salt, paprika, cayenne, and white pepper. Keep the sauce covered in a warm (not hot) place.

Note: Hollandaise sauce can be held for several hours in an earthenware crock in a warm spot on the back of the stove or in a stainless steel canister resting in a water bath at 125 degrees. Be aware that if the sauce becomes too cold or too hot, it may separate.

For the Oysters

1. Scrub the oyster shells with a stiff brush under cold running water. Using an oyster knife, pry open the oysters, discard the top shells, loosen the oyster from the bottom shell, and place the oysters on their half shells on a baking sheet. The oysters may be opened ahead of time and stored, covered, in the refrigerator for several hours.

2. Preheat the broiler to high.

3. Wash and stem the spinach. Melt the butter in a small skillet over medium-high heat. Add the spinach, season it with salt, sugar, and pepper and sauté until it is just wilted.

4. Tuck a few leaves of wilted spinach under each oyster. Douse each oyster with a little champagne.

5. Place the oysters under the hot broiler for about 30 to 60 seconds, until they are warmed through. They should still look almost raw.

6. Completely nap each oyster with champagne hollandaise sauce and place them back under the broiler until the sauce is golden brown, rotating the baking sheet so that the sauce will brown evenly on each oyster.

7. Carefully transfer the hot oysters to serving plates, spoon a dollop of caviar on the center of each one (if desired), and serve immediately.

A Crab Cake "Sandwich" with Fried Green Tomatoes and Tomato Vinaigrette

This dish is a celebration of summer and a great way to utilize green tomatoes from your garden. The Sweet Corn Relish can be made well in advance and is wonderfully versatile — perfect for a picnic or for an interesting accompaniment to any sandwich. The okra pickles are a snap to make and can be kept through the winter; they can be used as a novel cocktail garnish for Bloody Marys or martinis.

Serves 6

Crab Cakes

1 pound jumbo lump crabmeat

1 egg

7 tablespoons Dijon mustard

5 tablespoons mayonnaise

3 tablespoons freshly squeezed lemon juice

2 teaspoons Old Bay seasoning

½ teaspoon cayenne pepper

½ teaspoon celery salt

6 tablespoons peeled and finely chopped Roasted Red Pepper (see page 217)

For the Crab Cakes

1. Pick through the crabmeat carefully to be sure that all of the shell and cartilage are removed.

2. In a large mixing bowl, combine the egg, mustard, mayonnaise, lemon juice, Old Bay seasoning, cayenne, and celery salt. Using a rubber spatula, stir in the red pepper and celery leaves. Gently fold in the crabmeat and cracker crumbs, being careful not to break up the lumps of crabmeat. Season with kosher salt. Refrigerate for at least half an hour to allow the cracker crumbs to absorb some of the liquid.

3. Divide the crab mixture into 6 portions. Roll each one into a ball, dust with flour, and press lightly into a cake. The crab cakes may be prepared ahead of time, covered, and kept in the refrigerator for several hours until ready to cook.

4. In a large skillet, melt the butter over medium heat. Fry the crab cakes for 2 to 3 minutes on each side, until golden brown. Remove the crab cakes from the skillet and drain on paper towels.

Continued on page 90

Continued on page 90

2 tablespoons chopped celery leaves

1 cup cracker crumbs, preferably Ritz

Kosher salt to taste

½ cup all-purpose flour

¼ pound (1 stick) unsalted butter

Fried Green Tomatoes

1 cup all-purpose flour

1 tablespoon kosher salt

½ teaspoon freshly ground black
pepper

3 eggs

2 tablespoons water

2 cups Panko flakes (Japanese
breadcrumbs, sold in Asian markets)

1 tablespoon Cajun seasoning

3 large green tomatoes, cored and cut
into 12 quarter-inch slices

½ cup olive oil

To Serve

12 four-inch rosemary sprigs

1 recipe Tomato Vinaigrette
(see page 221)

1 recipe Sweet Corn Relish
(see page 170)

1 recipe Pickled Okra (optional,
see page 215)

1 recipe Waffle Potato Chips or good
quality potato chips (optional,
see page 221)

5. Keep the crab cakes warm in a low-temperature oven while you prepare the fried green tomatoes.

For the Fried Green Tomatoes

1. In a medium bowl, combine the flour, ½ tablespoon of the salt, and the pepper. In a second bowl, beat the eggs with 2 tablespoons of water. In a third bowl, combine the Panko flakes, Cajun seasoning, and the remaining salt.

2. Dredge each tomato slice in the seasoned flour until evenly coated, then into the egg mixture (allowing the excess egg to drip off), and, finally, into the seasoned breadcrumbs. Place the breaded tomato slices on a large plate or baking sheet. The breaded tomato slices may be prepared ahead of time and kept covered in the refrigerator for up to 4 hours.

3. In a large skillet, heat ¼ cup of the olive oil over high heat until almost smoking. Lower the heat to medium, carefully slip 6 of the breaded green tomato slices into the hot oil, and fry for 2 minutes on each side, or until golden brown. Remove the tomatoes from the pan and drain on paper towels. Keep warm in a low-temperature oven. Repeat with the remaining olive oil and tomato slices.

To Serve

1. Sandwich each crab cake between two slices of fried green tomato.

2. Slice each sandwich in half with a serrated knife and spear each half with a rosemary sprig.

3. Place a sandwich on each of 6 serving plates and splash the Tomato Vinaigrette around each sandwich. Garnish the sandwiches with a spoonful of Sweet Corn Relish, an okra pickle, and Waffle Potato Chips (if desired).

Mussels with Orecchiette

This is an elegant way to serve mussels out of their shells in combination with pasta. The orecchiette (Italian for "little ears") have an indentation that is just the right size to catch or hold a small mussel. The optional garnish of Crispy Collard Greens provides a striking contrast to the creamy white of the sauced pasta and adds a pleasant crunch to the sensual, tender textures of the dish. Keep the sauce a little thin, as it will continue to thicken on the pasta.

1. Throw away any mussels with broken shells. Scrub the mussels with a brush under cold running water and discard any that are not tightly closed.

2. In a saucepan large enough to hold all of the mussels after they open, bring the shallots, garlic, thyme, bay leaf, parsley, and wine or vermouth to a boil over high heat. Add the mussels, cover, and steam for about 3 minutes, or until the mussels just open. Transfer the mussels to a bowl and remove the shells.

3. Strain the mussel cooking liquid into a small saucepan and bring to a boil. Reduce by half and set aside. In another small saucepan, bring the cream to a boil, immediately reduce to a simmer, and reduce by half. Add about ¼ cup of the mussel liquid to the cream, adding more as needed to adjust the consistency and flavor of the sauce. Whisk in ½ cup of the cheese and season with salt, pepper, and a pinch of freshly grated nutmeg. Keep warm.

4. Bring a large pot of salted water to a boil and add the orecchiette. Cook the pasta for 8 to 10 minutes or until al dente. Drain and toss with extra virgin olive oil.

5. Bring the cream sauce to a simmer, add the mussels, and heat until warm. Add the orecchiette and stir to mix well. Adjust the seasonings. Spoon into 6 warm serving bowls, sprinkle with the remaining cheese, and garnish with Crispy Collard Greens.

Serves 6

1½ pounds (about 40) mussels

2 shallots, peeled and chopped

2 cloves garlic, minced

3 sprigs thyme

½ bay leaf

3 sprigs parsley

¾ cup dry white wine or vermouth

2 cups heavy cream

¾ cup finely grated Parmigiano-Reggiano cheese

Salt and freshly ground white pepper to taste

Freshly grated nutmeg to taste

½ pound dry orecchiette pasta

Extra virgin olive oil

Crispy Collard Greens (for garnish, see page 212)

Pecan-Crusted Softshell Crab Tempura

Softshell crabs are one of the greatest delicacies of our region. Every spring we look forward to coming up with new ways to serve them. The combination of crunchy, succulent textures and exciting flavors in this recipe is hard to beat. The preserved "Italian mustard fruit" is available in jars and may be found in many gourmet shops. (If it is unavailable, you may omit it.) The marinated cabbage slaw is wonderfully versatile and will undoubtedly become your favorite version of coleslaw once you try it. Fresh, live softshell crabs are worth waiting all year for. Frozen softshell crabs are not suitable for this preparation.

ℰᴑ

Serves 6

Marinated Cabbage Slaw

1 large head of cabbage, cored and sliced very thin

1 medium onion, cut in half and sliced very thin

1 cup white wine vinegar

¾ cup vegetable oil

1¼ cups sugar

1 tablespoon salt

1 tablespoon dry mustard

¾ tablespoon celery seed

½ cup chicken stock

Mustard-Butter Sauce

¼ cup white wine

¼ cup white wine vinegar

½ pound (2 sticks) unsalted butter, cut into 1-inch pieces

1½ tablespoons Dijon mustard

2 tablespoons finely chopped mustard fruits and 1 tablespoon of the syrup they are packed in

Salt to taste

Crabs

6 softshell crabs

3 quarts vegetable or peanut oil (for deep-frying)

1 recipe Tempura Batter (see page 220)

2 cups finely chopped pecans

Garnishes

Mustard fruits (for garnish)

Toasted pecan halves (for garnish)

For the Marinated Cabbage Slaw

1. In a stainless steel mixing bowl, layer the sliced cabbage and onion.

2. In a 2-quart saucepan, combine the vinegar, oil, sugar, salt, dry mustard, celery seed, and chicken stock and bring to a boil.

3. Pour the hot liquid over the cabbage and onion but do not mix.

4. Cover tightly with plastic wrap and marinate for 6 to 8 hours or overnight in the refrigerator. Toss before serving. The cabbage slaw can be made several days in advance and stored in the refrigerator until ready to use.

For the Mustard-Butter Sauce

1. In a 2-quart saucepan over medium-high heat, combine the white wine and white wine vinegar. Boil until the mixture is syrupy and has reduced to about 2 tablespoons.

2. Reduce the heat to low and whisk in the butter, incorporating one piece of butter before adding the next. Continue until all of the butter is used up.

3. Remove from heat and whisk in the mustard. Stir in the chopped mustard fruits and syrup.

4. Season with a pinch of salt. Keep warm (not hot) until ready to serve.

For the Crabs

1. Clean the crabs by lifting up the side flaps and pulling out the feathery gills. Remove the flap underneath. Rinse in cold water and dry on paper towels.

2. In a deep fryer or heavy pot, heat the oil to 350 degrees.

3. Dip each crab into the Tempura Batter and sprinkle the crab with pecans.

4. Carefully (because the crabs tend to "pop" and splatter) slip the crabs into the hot oil, turn them with a slotted spoon, and fry for 3 to 4 minutes, until they are golden brown. Remove the crabs from the oil and drain them on paper towels.

To Serve

1. Make a nest of marinated cabbage slaw on each plate. Place one crab on top of each pile of slaw.

2. Using a spoon or ladle, pool the mustard-butter sauce around each crab. Garnish with thin slices of mustard fruit and pecan halves.

Truffle-Dusted Maine Diver's Scallops on Cauliflower Puree

If you have access to large, impeccably fresh sea scallops, this dish will astonish you with its sensuality and simplicity. We use what are called Maine "diver's scallops" (available at high-end grocery stores) — meaning they are harvested by divers and not stored for long periods on deep-sea fishing boats in chemical preservatives. Frozen sea scallops release too much water when you try to sear them and will not work well when cooked this way. When black truffles are not in season, we substitute black sesame seeds with surprisingly good results.

The sea scallops are rolled in minced truffles (or sesame seeds), seared in a hot pan until lightly crusted, and placed on a bed of cauliflower puree. Most people swoon at their first taste of the cauliflower — never guessing that this lowly vegetable could taste so sublime when pureed with a little potato, cream, and butter. (The puree is wonderfully versatile and also makes a great vegetable accompaniment for roast meats.)

For the Cauliflower Puree

1. Place the potato in a pot of cold salted water. Bring to a boil, add the cauliflower, and cook until the vegetables are very soft, about 7 to 10 minutes. Drain well.

2. Using a food processor, puree the potato and cauliflower, scraping down the sides with a rubber spatula as needed. Add the cream, butter, salt, pepper, and nutmeg.

For the Scallops

1. Soak the scallops in ice water for 3 minutes. Dry the scallops on paper towels, season with salt and pepper, and roll the scallops in the truffle or sesame seeds to coat them on all sides.

2. In a nonstick pan, heat the clarified butter over medium-high heat. Carefully add the coated scallops to the hot pan and cook until they are golden brown on both sides. Do not overcook.

To Serve

1. Spoon a few tablespoons of cauliflower puree onto the center of each of 6 plates. Place a seared scallop on top of the puree.

2. Slice each scallop in half, exposing the pearly white center.

3. Garnish with an Herbed Potato Crisp (if desired) and drizzle the Red Wine Butter Sauce around the puree.

Serves 6

Cauliflower Puree

1 small Idaho potato, peeled and roughly chopped

2 cups cauliflower florets

2 tablespoons heavy cream

1 tablespoon butter

Salt and freshly ground white pepper to taste

Pinch of freshly ground nutmeg

Scallops

6 large, fresh sea scallops

Salt and freshly ground black pepper to taste

¼ cup minced black truffle or whole black sesame seeds

2 tablespoons clarified butter

To Serve

6 Herbed Potato Crisps (optional, see page 213)

½ cup Red Wine Butter Sauce (see page 216)

Scallop, Ham, and Pineapple "Sandwiches"

A large sea scallop is seared, sliced crosswise, and layered with a slice of ham and fresh pineapple, forming a little sandwich. The natural sweetness of the scallops is accentuated by the juicy pineapple and offset by the rich saltiness of the country ham. The presentation is made more whimsical by the accompaniments of Shoestring Potatoes, pineapple relish, and a "frilled toothpick" in the form of a sprig of fresh rosemary.

Serves 6

Pineapple Relish

1 cup finely diced fresh pineapple

1 teaspoon finely diced red onion

¼ teaspoon finely minced jalapeño pepper

1 teaspoon finely chopped, fresh cilantro leaves

2 tablespoons extra virgin olive oil

Salt and freshly ground black pepper to taste

Sugar to taste

Scallop Sandwiches

2 tablespoons vegetable oil

¼ fresh pineapple, peeled and cored and cut into ⅛-inch-thick slices

6 very large sea scallops

Salt and freshly ground white pepper to taste

3 slices country ham, cut into 1½-inch squares

12 four-inch rosemary sprigs

To Serve

Sweet-and-Sour Fish Sauce (see page 220)

Shoestring Potatoes (see page 170)

For the Pineapple Relish

In a small mixing bowl, combine the pineapple, onion, jalapeño pepper, cilantro, and olive oil. Season with salt, pepper, and sugar. The relish may be prepared in advance and stored in the refrigerator overnight.

For the Scallop Sandwiches

1. In a nonstick pan, heat 1 tablespoon of the vegetable oil. Add the pineapple slices and cook until they are golden on both sides, then remove and keep warm.

2. Season the scallops with salt and white pepper.

3. In the same nonstick pan, heat the remaining vegetable oil over high heat. Add the scallops to the hot pan and cook until they are golden brown on both sides. Do not overcook.

4. Slice the scallops in half crosswise. Sandwich a slice of pineapple and country ham between the two halves of each scallop. Using a serrated knife, slice each scallop sandwich in half and spear each half with a sprig of fresh rosemary.

To Serve

1. Place a scallop sandwich in the center of each serving plate and splash the Sweet-and-Sour Fish Sauce around the plate.

2. Garnish with pineapple relish and Shoestring Potatoes.

Fricassee of Maine Lobster with Potato Gnocchi and Curried Walnuts

A fricassee is usually a "light stew" and is often made with sautéed chicken or veal and served in a creamy sauce. This version, which uses chopped lobster knuckles and tails, is meant to resemble a stew.

The ethereal potato gnocchi are seductive in a number of ways. The little dumplings are particularly intriguing in this dish because they echo the shape and texture of the lobster knuckle meat. The sweet peeled green grapes and savory pearl onions accentuate the succulence of the lobster, while the walnuts, accented with a hint of curry, add crunch. And, yes, the amount of butter in this dish is sinful — but sublime.

Serves 6

Potato Gnocchi

2 Idaho potatoes, unpeeled

½ to ¾ cup all-purpose flour

Salt and freshly ground black pepper to taste

1 egg yolk, beaten

For the Potato Gnocchi

1. Preheat the oven to 350 degrees.

2. Bake the potatoes for about 1 hour, or until they are very tender and the skins are crisp. (Do not overbake.)

3. While the potatoes are still warm, sprinkle a little of the flour on a work surface. Peel the potatoes and pass them through a food mill onto the floured surface. Sprinkle the potatoes with ½ cup of the flour, salt, and pepper and knead to form a dough. Make a well in the middle of the dough and add the beaten egg yolk. Knead until the egg is completely combined, adding more flour as necessary until the dough is smooth.

4. On a clean work surface, roll the dough into long even logs, about ½ inch in diameter. Cut the logs into 1-inch pieces to form the gnocchi. Pinch the middle of each gnocchi to form its distinctive hourglass shape.

5. Bring a large pot of salted water to a boil. Meanwhile, fill a large mixing bowl with cold water and ice cubes.

6. Add the gnocchi to the boiling water, reduce the heat, and simmer for 5 minutes. Drain and plunge the gnocchi into ice water. Allow the gnocchi to cool completely in the ice water and drain. Transfer them to a baking sheet lined with parchment or waxed paper and blot them dry with paper towels. The gnocchi may be prepared in advance and stored, covered with plastic wrap, for up to 2 days in the refrigerator.

Curried Walnuts

1 tablespoon butter

¼ pound walnut halves

1 teaspoon curry powder

2 tablespoons sugar

½ teaspoon salt

For the Curried Walnuts

1. In a large skillet melt the butter over medium-high heat until it begins to foam.

2. Add the walnuts and cook for about 3 minutes, stirring constantly, until the walnuts are well toasted and lightly colored. Add the curry powder, sugar, and salt, and cook for 1 more minute.

3. Pour the walnuts onto a wire rack placed over a baking sheet. Let cool to room temperature.

4. Store in an airtight container at room temperature until ready to serve.

For the Lobster

1. In a large skillet, heat the clarified butter over medium-high heat. Add the gnocchi and mushrooms and cook until they are golden brown. Transfer the gnocchi and mushrooms to a plate.

2. Return the skillet to medium heat, add the Vegetable Stock, and reduce it by half. Reduce the heat to low and, piece by piece, whisk in the butter. Add the peeled grapes, pearl onions, lobster meat, and the potato gnocchi and mushroom mixture, allowing them to warm through. Season with salt and pepper to taste.

To Serve

1. Using a slotted spoon, divide the lobster and gnocchi mixture among 6 serving plates.

2. Drizzle a little of the pan sauce over each portion and garnish with curried walnuts.

Lobster

2 tablespoons clarified butter

36 gnocchi

1 cup tiny white button mushrooms

½ cup Vegetable Stock (see page 221)

½ pound (2 sticks) butter, cut into cubes

18 peeled green grapes

18 pearl onions, blanched and peeled

2 cups cooked lobster knuckle or tail meat, cut into 1-inch pieces

Salt and freshly ground black pepper to taste

Pan-Roasted Maine Lobster
with Rosemary Cream

This is one of our favorite ways to serve lobster. The rich, flavorful sauce perfumed with rosemary tastes as though it took days to make, when in fact it is a quick reduction of tomato juice, stock, cream, and brandy made in the same pan used to roast the lobster tails. While we offer half a lobster as a first course, the preparation works equally well as a main course using a whole lobster.

Serves 6

3 live lobsters, about 1½ pounds each

¼ cup vegetable oil

2 tablespoons brandy

¾ cup Vegetable Stock (see page 221)

¼ cup tomato or V8 juice

¼ cup dry vermouth

½ cup heavy cream

2 tablespoons julienned celery

2 tablespoons julienned green onion

2 tablespoons julienned carrot

1 tablespoon fresh rosemary, stems removed

Salt and freshly ground black pepper to taste

&

To Cook the Lobster Claws

1. Hold the lobsters with a kitchen towel and carefully pull off the claws and tails. (Discard the bodies or keep them to flavor a lobster stock or soup.)

2. In a large kettle or steamer, bring 2 inches of salted water to a rolling boil. Add the claws, cover, and cook for 8 minutes.

3. Remove the claws from the steamer and plunge them into ice water to stop the cooking. Remove the claws from the ice water.

4. Using a mallet, carefully crack the claws and knuckles and remove the meat. Reserve the claw and knuckle meat in the refrigerator until ready to use.

To Cook the Lobster Tails and Make the Sauce

1. Using a sharp knife, cut through the center of the shells, dividing the raw tails in half lengthwise. Leave the meat in the shells.

2. In a sauté pan with a tight-fitting lid, heat the vegetable oil over high heat until almost smoking. Add the lobster tails in their shells (shell side down), cover, and cook for 3 minutes.

3. Remove the pan from the heat, uncover, and add the brandy. Return to heat and cook for 1 minute more. Add the stock, tomato or V8 juice, and vermouth and cook for 2 minutes. Add the cream, claw and knuckle meat, celery, onion, carrot, and rosemary and cook another minute. Season with salt and pepper.

To Serve

1. Using a fork, loosen, but do not remove, each lobster tail from its shell.

2. Place ½ lobster tail (in its shell) in the center of each of 6 plates; place a claw on top of each tail.

3. Spoon the cream sauce, lobster knuckles, and julienned vegetables on top of and around the lobster tail and claw.

Red Mullet with Gazpacho Sauce and Black Olive Tapenade

All of the flavors and colors of the Mediterranean are captured in this wonderfully delicate little first course. While the red mullet, or rouget (now available in some fish markets), has a unique rose-gold skin when cooked, any delicate white fish, such as sole, flounder, or rockfish, will lend itself nicely to this preparation. If the skin is cooked crisply, it adds a pleasant textural note, but if you prefer, use a skinless fillet. The fish is nested on top of a mound of garden vegetables and surrounded by a pool of gazpacho rimmed with olive oil. A crouton of black olive tapenade accentuates the bold flavors and colors of the dish.

∽

Serves 6

Gazpacho Sauce

3½ pounds red ripe tomatoes, cored and coarsely chopped

½ cucumber, peeled, seeded, and coarsely chopped

1 red bell pepper, seeded and chopped

½ jalapeño pepper, seeded and chopped

½ medium onion, coarsely chopped, preferably Vidalia

2 stalks celery, coarsely chopped

½ teaspoon minced garlic

3 tablespoons extra virgin olive oil

½ teaspoon Tabasco

1 tablespoon fresh lemon juice

1 tablespoon rice wine vinegar

1 teaspoon sugar

½ teaspoon ground cumin

½ teaspoon celery salt

Salt and freshly ground black pepper to taste

Gazpacho Salsa

1 tablespoon peeled, seeded, and minced tomato

1 tablespoon peeled, seeded, and minced cucumber

1 tablespoon seeded and minced red bell pepper

1 tablespoon seeded and minced green bell pepper

1 tablespoon seeded and minced yellow bell pepper

For the Gazpacho Sauce

1. In a blender or food processor, puree the tomato, cucumber, bell pepper, jalapeño pepper, onion, celery, and garlic in batches until smooth. Strain.

2. Add the olive oil, Tabasco, lemon juice, vinegar, sugar, cumin, and celery salt. Mix well and refrigerate. When the puree is thoroughly chilled, season to taste with salt and pepper. Store in the refrigerator until ready to serve and allow to come to room temperature before serving.

Note: Makes about five cups. You will need approximately 1 cup for this recipe. Serve the remainder as a soup the following day.

For the Gazpacho Salsa

1. In a small mixing bowl, combine the tomato, cucumber, bell peppers, jalapeño pepper, red onion, and shallot.

2. Stir in the parsley, tarragon, celery salt, extra virgin olive oil, and sherry vinegar.

3. Season with salt and pepper, and refrigerate.

For the Croutons

1. Preheat the broiler.

2. Cut out 6 rounds of bread, about 2 inches in diameter, and place them on a baking sheet.

3. Toast the bread rounds under the broiler on both sides.

4. Spoon the olive tapenade on the toasts and set aside.

For the Fish

1. In a nonstick skillet, heat the oil over high heat.

2. Season the fish on both sides with salt and pepper.

3. Cook the fish, skin side down, for about 2 minutes, until the edges are crisp and golden.

4. Flip the fillets and finish cooking them on the other side for about 30 seconds. Keep warm.

To Serve

1. Pour 2 tablespoons of the gazpacho sauce into each of 6 serving bowls. Drizzle a small amount of extra virgin olive oil around the sauce. Place 1 tablespoon of gazpacho salsa in the center of each bowl.

2. Place 1 hot fish fillet on top of the salsa and lay a crouton of black olive tapenade on each one.

1 teaspoon seeded and minced jalapeño pepper

1 tablespoon minced red onion

1 teaspoon minced shallot

1 teaspoon very finely chopped fresh parsley

1 teaspoon finely chopped fresh tarragon

¼ teaspoon celery salt

1 tablespoon extra virgin olive oil

1 tablespoon sherry vinegar

Salt and freshly ground black pepper to taste

Croutons

2 pieces thinly sliced white bread

2 tablespoons black olive tapenade (available jarred in gourmet food shops)

Fish

1 tablespoon vegetable oil

6 red mullet fillets, about 3 ounces each (skin on, scaled)

Salt and freshly ground black pepper to taste

Garnish

2 tablespoons extra virgin olive oil

Lemon and Black Pepper Risotto

This vibrant, refreshing, and lemony risotto can be made in advance, refrigerated for several days, and finished in a few minutes just before serving. It makes a wonderful first course, or it can be served as an accompaniment to grilled fish or chicken.

For the Risotto Base

1. In a 2-quart saucepan, bring the stock or water to a boil over high heat. Reduce the heat and keep the stock just below boiling.

2. In another 2-quart saucepan, heat the butter and oil. Add the onion and cook until translucent.

3. Add the rice and stir until it is evenly coated with the butter-oil mixture.

4. Slowly add the hot stock to the rice, ⅔ cup at a time, stirring constantly until the rice absorbs the liquid. This should take about 4 to 5 minutes for each addition.

5. When all the stock has been absorbed, remove the risotto from the stove and pour onto a baking sheet to stop the cooking and cool as quickly as possible. (The rice will still taste a bit raw in the center.) Refrigerate, uncovered, until cold. The risotto base can then be stored in a covered plastic container for up to 2 days.

To Finish and Serve the Risotto

1. Bring the stock or water to a boil.

2. Place the chilled risotto in a 4-quart saucepan over medium heat. Pour 1½ cups of the boiling stock slowly into the risotto, stirring constantly with a wooden spoon. Continue cooking until the rice is just barely tender but still al dente.

3. Stir in the cheese and butter, adjusting the consistency with more stock if the risotto becomes too thick. Season with salt and coarsely ground black pepper. Remove from heat and add the lemon juice and zest.

4. Divide the risotto into 6 warm soup plates and garnish with celery leaves.

Serves 6

Risotto Base

2 cups chicken stock, Vegetable Stock (see page 221), or water

2 tablespoons butter

2 tablespoons olive oil

½ large onion, minced

1 cup Arborio rice

To Finish and Serve the Risotto

1½ cups (approximately) chicken stock, Vegetable Stock (see page 221), or water

1 cup freshly grated Parmesan cheese

2 tablespoons butter

Salt and coarsely ground black pepper to taste

2 tablespoons lemon juice

1 tablespoon lemon zest

Pale green leaves of celery hearts (for garnish)

Shrimp and Corn Risotto

Sweet corn and rice are a marriage made in heaven. The kernels of corn mimic the texture of the rice, while the addition of a corn puree adds a rich, natural creaminess to this risotto. The risotto base can be made in advance, kept in the refrigerator for several days, and finished in just a few minutes before serving. While the shrimps enhance both the texture and natural sweetness of the risotto, they can easily be omitted, making the dish an ideal vegetarian option.

ℰↄ

Serves 6

Risotto Base

4 ears fresh corn

2 cups chicken stock, Vegetable Stock (see page 221), or water

2 tablespoons butter

2 tablespoons olive oil

½ large onion, minced

1 cup Arborio rice

Corn Puree

1½ cups Vegetable Stock (see page 221)

1½ cups corn kernels (reserved from previous procedure)

For the Risotto Base

1. Shuck the corn, brushing off all the silk. Using a sharp knife, strip the corn kernels from the cobs. Reserve the kernels and the cobs separately. (You should have about 3 cups of corn kernels.)

2. In a 2-quart saucepan, bring the stock or water and corn cobs to a boil over high heat. Reduce the heat to simmer.

3. In another 2-quart saucepan, heat the butter and oil. Add the onion and cook until translucent. Add the rice and stir until it is evenly coated with the butter-oil mixture.

4. Slowly add the hot stock, ⅔ cup at a time, stirring constantly until the rice absorbs the liquid. This should take about 4 to 5 minutes for each addition.

5. When all the stock has been absorbed, remove the risotto from the stove and pour onto a baking sheet to stop the cooking and cool as quickly as possible. (The rice will still taste a bit raw in the center.) Refrigerate, uncovered, until cold. The risotto base can then be stored in a covered plastic container for up to 2 days.

For the Corn Puree

1. In a small saucepan, bring the stock to a boil. Add the corn kernels and cook for about 5 minutes, or until they are tender.

2. Transfer the stock and corn to a blender and puree until smooth.

For the Risotto, Shrimp, and Corn

1. Bring the stock or water to a boil.

2. Place the chilled risotto and corn kernels in a 4-quart saucepan over medium heat. Pour 1½ cups of the boiling stock slowly into the risotto, stirring constantly with a wooden spoon. Continue cooking until the rice is just barely tender but still al dente.

3. Stir in the cheese, corn puree, and 2 tablespoons of the butter, adjusting the consistency with more stock if the risotto becomes too thick. Season with salt, pepper, and nutmeg. Remove from heat and keep warm.

4. In a 10-inch sauté pan, heat the oil over medium-high heat. Add the shrimp and sauté until just pink, being careful not to overcook. Add the remaining butter, shallot, and garlic, and sauté for a few seconds more. Season with salt and pepper, remove from the pan, and keep warm.

To Serve

Divide the risotto into 6 warm soup plates. Arrange 6 pieces of shrimp on top of each portion. Garnish with the cheese, Frizzled Leeks, and chives.

Risotto, Shrimp, and Corn

1½ cups (approximately) chicken stock, Vegetable Stock (see page 221), or water

1½ cups reserved corn kernels

1 cup freshly grated Parmesan cheese

½ cup corn puree

3 tablespoons butter

Salt and freshly ground black pepper to taste

Freshly grated nutmeg to taste

2 tablespoons olive oil

18 fresh shrimp, peeled, deveined, and split in half lengthwise

1 teaspoon minced shallot

1 teaspoon minced garlic

Garnishes

Freshly grated Parmesan cheese

Frizzled Leeks (optional, see page 213)

1 tablespoon chopped fresh chives

Macaroni and Cheese with Virginia Country Ham

This is a suave and sophisticated reincarnation of an old childhood favorite. Every bit as comforting and soul satisfying as mother's, this delicate version is actually easier to prepare. All of the preparation can be done in advance and finished just before serving. We use a well-aged Dutch Gouda cheese, which has the consistency of Parmesan. In the restaurant, we serve the macaroni in individual Parmesan tuile *baskets and shave fragrant white truffles over the pasta at the table.*

ℰ✄

1. In a large pot, bring 4 quarts of salted water to a boil. Add the macaroni and cook until the pasta is half done; the interior will be slightly raw. Drain the pasta and place it in a small bowl. Add the olive oil and toss to keep the macaroni from sticking together. Allow it to cool. The macaroni can be made the day before and kept in the refrigerator until needed.

2. In a 4-quart saucepan over medium-low heat, melt the butter. Add the garlic and shallot and sweat for 5 minutes, stirring occasionally, being careful not to brown them. Add the cream, bring to a rapid boil, then reduce the heat and simmer. Cook, stirring, until the cream has reduced by one quarter and coats the back of a spoon.

3. Whisk in the grated cheeses and cook for a minute or so, or until the cheese is melted and the mixture is smooth. Season with nutmeg, salt, and pepper. Remove from heat and pass through a fine strainer (optional). At this point, the sauce can be refrigerated for a day or two.

4. Return the cheese sauce to the pan over low heat and add the already cooked macaroni. Simmer for a minute or two to make sure the pasta is warmed through.

To Serve

1. Place a Lacy Parmesan Wafer basket (see page 46) in the center of each of 4 warmed plates.

2. Spoon about ½ cup of the pasta onto each wafer.

3. Ladle 1 or 2 tablespoons of the cheese sauce around the plate and garnish each portion with the julienned ham, chopped chives, and Crispy Fried Onions. If you like, white truffle can be shaved on the macaroni at the table.

Serves 4

¾ cup macaroni or your favorite tubular pasta

1 tablespoon olive oil

2 tablespoons butter

½ teaspoon minced garlic

½ tablespoon minced shallot

2 cups heavy cream

½ cup freshly grated aged Gouda cheese

¼ cup freshly grated Parmesan cheese

Pinch of freshly grated nutmeg

Salt and freshly ground black pepper to taste

Garnishes

4 Lacy Parmesan Wafers formed into baskets (see page 46)

2 slices Virginia country ham, finely julienned

2 teaspoons finely chopped chives

Crispy Fried Onions (see page 213)

White truffle (optional)

Shrimp with White Bean Salad and Italian Sausage

This is a rustic Italian-inspired combination of shrimp, roasted peppers, beans, and sausage that is best served at room temperature. The unexpected hint of orange brightens the flavors of the dish and complements both the shrimp and sausage. This is a robust first course for a simple summer supper and ideal for a buffet or picnic because it can be prepared well in advance.

℘

For the White Bean Salad

1. Place the beans in an 8-quart saucepan and cover with cold water. Soak overnight.

2. Drain the beans, cover with fresh salted water, and cook over medium heat for about 1 hour, or until just barely tender.

3. In a large mixing bowl, combine the beans, celery, oranges, tomatoes, cilantro, garlic, olive oil, and balsamic vinegar. Season to taste with salt and pepper.

For the Shrimp

1. Combine the orange juice, orange zest, olive oil, garlic, cayenne pepper, and soy sauce in a mixing bowl. Add the shrimp and marinate for 15 minutes.

2. Preheat the grill to medium-high heat.

3. Remove the shrimp from the marinade and grill for 2 to 3 minutes, or until they are just cooked through.

To Serve and Garnish

1. Preheat the oven to 350 degrees.

2. In a large oven-proof skillet, brown the sausages over medium heat, then place the skillet in the oven and cook the sausages about 10 to 15 minutes. Drain the sausages on paper towels and slice each one on the bias into ½-inch slices.

3. Mound ½ cup white bean salad in the center of each plate. Arrange the slices of Italian sausage and shrimp on top of the beans and garnish each plate with Roasted Red Peppers, parsley, chives, and celery leaves.

Serves 8

White Bean Salad

1 pound dried cannellini beans

3 celery stalks, minced

3 oranges, rind and pith removed, sectioned

¾ cup peeled, chopped fresh tomatoes

¼ cup finely chopped fresh cilantro

2 teaspoons finely minced garlic

¼ cup olive oil

⅓ cup balsamic vinegar

Salt and freshly ground black pepper to taste

Shrimp

Juice and zest of 1 orange

¼ cup olive oil

4 large garlic cloves, very finely minced

½ teaspoon cayenne pepper

¼ cup soy sauce

24 large fresh shrimp, peeled

To Serve and Garnish

4 sweet Italian sausages

2 Roasted Red Peppers (see page 217), roughly cut into 1-inch squares

Parsley leaves (for garnish)

Snipped chives (for garnish)

Celery heart leaves (for garnish)

Salads, Cheeses, and Intermezzos

A Burst of Camembert on Baby Greens

It is always a dilemma when deciding whether or not to offer a cheese course as part of a formal dinner. While always welcomed by wine lovers, cheese can sometimes overly extend a meal. This dish provides a unique way to combine a salad and a cheese course before dessert.

The little wedges of phyllo-wrapped cheese can be assembled well in advance and browned just before serving. When you cut into the pastry with a fork, the warm cheese bursts out onto the greens, creating a delightful surprise. The richness of the cheese is beautifully balanced with the tartness of the balsamic vinegar. We sometimes accompany this dish with a glass of aged Madeira.

ℰℭ

For the Camembert Triangles

1. Line a baking sheet with parchment paper.

2. Cut the wheel of Camembert into 6 triangles.

3. On a cutting board, lay out one sheet of phyllo dough and brush it with melted butter. (Keep the remaining phyllo covered with a moistened tea towel.)

4. Place another sheet of phyllo on top of the first and brush it with butter, reserving about 4 tablespoons of the butter.

5. Using a sharp knife, cut the buttered phyllo sheets into 6 strips, about 2½ inches wide.

6. Place a triangle of Camembert on one end of each phyllo strip. Fold one corner of the dough over to cover the cheese and form a triangle. Continue folding the dough, like a flag, maintaining the triangular shape. Place the triangles, seam side down, on the baking sheet and refrigerate until ready to serve.

To Serve

1. In a small heavy-bottomed saucepan, reduce the balsamic vinegar by half and set aside.

2. In a large skillet, heat about 4 tablespoons of the remaining melted butter over low heat. Add the pastry-wrapped cheese pieces and cook for 30 to 45 seconds on each side until just golden brown. Using tongs, remove the cheese triangles from the skillet and drain on paper towels.

3. Place the greens in a large bowl, lightly dress them with the Sherry Vinaigrette, and place a small mound of dressed greens in the center of each plate.

4. Place a warm cheese triangle on top of each pile of greens. Drizzle the reduced balsamic vinegar around the greens and garnish with the pecans. Serve immediately.

Serves 6

Camembert Triangles

1 small wheel (about 9 ounces) Camembert, chilled

2 sheets phyllo dough

¼ pound (1 stick) butter, melted

To Serve

½ cup balsamic vinegar

2 cups assorted baby greens, washed and dried

¼ cup Sherry Vinaigrette (see page 218)

Toasted pecans (for garnish)

Quince Preserves

At The Inn we present our cheeses on a rolling cow named Faira. This simple quince preserve has become a favorite accompaniment for our cheese course. In Spain, it is traditionally served with manchego *cheese. We also serve it with chilled foie gras and a little toasted brioche.*

છ૭

1. Roughly chop half of the quince, including the peels and cores. Place the chopped fruit and 4 cups of water in a heavy-bottomed saucepan. Bring the mixture to a boil over low heat and simmer for 30 to 40 minutes, or until the fruit is very tender.

2. Pour the fruit mixture into a damp jelly bag or fine mesh sieve set over a large bowl and drain for 12 hours or overnight.

3. In a heavy-bottomed saucepan, cook the drained quince juice and sugar over low heat, stirring frequently, until the sugar is dissolved.

4. While the quince juice is cooking, peel, core, and thinly slice the remaining 2 pounds of quince. Bring the juice mixture to a boil and add the sliced quince and lemon juice. Simmer the fruit, skimming any foam that comes to the surface, for 30 minutes, or until it is tender. Bring the mixture back to a boil and cook until it is syrupy and deep red in color, or until a candy thermometer registers 224 degrees.

5. Pour the preserves into sterile glass jars or airtight storage containers and chill until ready to serve. For longer storage, the preserves may be frozen.

Makes 4 cups

4 pounds quince

4 cups sugar

¼ cup lemon juice

Warm Salad of Grilled Asparagus and Prawns with Sherry Vinaigrette

I love the idea of a warm salad, because the flavors, like those of a fine cheese, become more pronounced when the dish is served warm. The French call the concept a salade tiède, *meaning "lukewarm," but unfortunately, no elegant and appetizing parallel English descriptive adjective yet exists.*

Grilling imparts an added dimension of flavor to asparagus. For this recipe, we prefer jumbo or super-colossal asparagus, which we boil briefly and then refresh in ice water before grilling. This preserves the vegetable's vibrant green color and ensures that it will be uniformly cooked. While we use freshwater prawns because their tender texture echoes that of the asparagus, regular shrimp will work as well.

For the Grilled Asparagus

1. Preheat the grill to high.
2. Bring a large pot of salted water to a boil. Fill a mixing bowl with ice water and set aside.
3. Add the asparagus to the rapidly boiling water and cook for about 3 to 4 minutes, or until the asparagus spears are just tender. Remove the spears and immediately refresh them in the ice water until well chilled. Drain thoroughly.
4. Marinate the asparagus in the olive oil, bay leaf, and garlic. This can be prepared in advance and stored in the refrigerator overnight.
5. Place the marinated asparagus on the grill and cook for about 1 minute on each side until the spears are marked by the grill and warmed through.
6. Remove the asparagus from the grill, place them in a large mixing bowl, toss with the Sherry Vinaigrette, and season with salt and pepper. Keep warm.

For the Prawns

1. Season the prawns with salt and pepper.
2. In a 10-inch skillet, heat the vegetable oil over high heat until almost smoking. Place the prawns in the skillet, turn the heat to medium, and cook for about 1 minute.
3. Add the butter, shallot, garlic, and tarragon and continue to cook for another minute, or until just pink.
4. Remove the prawns from the pan and keep warm.

To Serve and Garnish

1. Place 3 grilled asparagus spears in the center of each of 4 large plates.
2. Sprinkle the asparagus with chopped egg, ribbons of ham, capers, and mushrooms.
3. Place ¼ of the prawns or shrimp on top of each serving.
4. Drizzle each plate with a few drops of extra virgin olive oil and balsamic vinegar.

Serves 4

Grilled Asparagus

12 jumbo asparagus, trimmed and peeled

2 tablespoons extra virgin olive oil

1 bay leaf, crushed

½ tablespoon minced garlic

½ cup Sherry Vinaigrette (see page 218)

Salt and freshly ground black pepper to taste

Prawns

6 extra-large blue prawns or ¾ pound fresh shrimp, peeled and split lengthwise

Salt and freshly ground black pepper to taste

¼ cup vegetable oil

1 tablespoon butter

½ tablespoon chopped shallot

1 teaspoon chopped garlic

1 tablespoon chopped fresh tarragon

Garnishes

1 hard-boiled egg, roughly chopped

3 slices country ham, cut into fettuccine-size ribbons

1 tablespoon capers, drained

½ cup white button mushrooms, cut into small matchsticks

2 tablespoons extra virgin olive oil

1 tablespoon aged balsamic vinegar

Brussels Sprout Petals with Coriander Vinaigrette and Pickled Cranberries

Many people seem to have negative feelings toward Brussels sprouts, usually because the name conjures up memories of odiferous and overcooked little cabbages. Even one with a distaste for Brussels sprouts will enjoy this version of the vegetable as a salad. The secret to cooking the sprouts is wonderfully simple. The petals are removed and cooked for less than a minute until they turn a brilliant green. Most people have never tried them this way and will not even recognize them. Tossed with Pickled Cranberries, they make a colorful accompaniment for a buffet platter of cold roast beef, lamb, or chicken.

&

For the Brussels Sprout Petals

1. With a paring knife, trim the ends off the Brussels sprouts and peel away the leaves (like removing the petals from a rose).

2. Meanwhile, bring a large pot of salted water to a boil. Fill a mixing bowl with ice water and set aside.

3. Add the Brussels sprout petals to the rapidly boiling water and cook for about 20 seconds. (They will turn bright green.) Do not overcook. Drain the petals through a colander and plunge them into the ice water. Allow the leaves to chill completely. Lift them out of the water, drain, and store in the refrigerator until ready to serve.

For the Coriander Vinaigrette

1. In a spice grinder or pepper mill, grind the coriander and fennel.

2. Meanwhile, in a medium-size saucepan, combine the vermouth or wine, onion, garlic, white wine vinegar, and ½ cup of water. Bring to a boil over medium heat and then remove the pot from the heat.

3. Add the olive oil, lemon juice, thyme, bay leaf, cracked black pepper, and ground coriander and fennel to the vermouth and vinegar mixture. Stir and cool to room temperature. Adjust the seasoning if necessary. The vinaigrette can be made up to 2 days ahead of time and stored, covered, in the refrigerator. Allow it to come back to room temperature, remove and discard the bay leaf, and shake well before serving.

To Serve

1. In a small skillet, cook the bacon over medium-high heat until crisp. Drain the bacon on paper towels.

2. In a large salad bowl, toss the Brussels sprout petals, bacon, and Pickled Cranberries with the coriander vinaigrette. Divide the salad among 8 plates and sprinkle with the toasted fennel and coriander seeds, if desired.

Serves 8

Brussels Sprout Petals

2 pounds Brussels sprouts, washed

Coriander Vinaigrette

1 teaspoon coriander seeds

½ teaspoon fennel seeds

½ cup dry vermouth or white wine

1 onion, finely chopped

3 cloves garlic, minced

1 teaspoon white wine vinegar

3 tablespoons extra virgin olive oil

1 tablespoon fresh lemon juice

½ teaspoon chopped fresh thyme leaves

½ bay leaf

½ teaspoon cracked black pepper

Salt and freshly ground black pepper to taste

Garnishes

2 thick slices bacon, cut into ½-inch pieces

1 cup Pickled Cranberries (see page 215)

½ teaspoon toasted fennel seeds (optional)

½ teaspoon toasted coriander seeds (optional)

Endive Salad with Pomegranate Vinaigrette and Lemon Cream

In the winter, when delicate salad greens are hard to come by, we love the crunchy combination of crisp pale-green Belgian endive sprinkled with ruby-red pomegranate seeds. This dressy, easy-to-make, and colorful salad is a festive addition to an elegant holiday dinner.

&

Serves 6

Pomegranate Vinaigrette

1 pomegranate

½ cup raspberry vinegar

½ tablespoon dry mustard

½ cup olive oil

¾ cup vegetable oil

½ tablespoon chopped shallot

½ tablespoon chives

Salt and freshly ground black pepper
to taste

Lemon Cream

¼ cup crème fraîche

¼ cup heavy cream

1 tablespoon fresh lemon juice

Salt, freshly ground white pepper,
and sugar to taste

To Serve

6 heads Belgian endive, trimmed and
pulled apart into spears

½ cup pomegranate vinaigrette

Chervil sprigs (for garnish)

Chopped chives (for garnish)

¼ cup pomegranate seeds (for garnish,
reserved from the pomegranate
vinaigrette)

For the Pomegranate Vinaigrette

1. Using the palm of your hand, roll the pomegranate over a hard surface to loosen the seeds. Cut the pomegranate in half crosswise. Hold half of the pomegranate, cut side down, over a large mixing bowl and remove the seeds by tapping the fruit firmly with a wooden spoon. Remove any membranes that are released while tapping out the seeds. Reserve the seeds for the vinaigrette and for garnishing the salad just before serving. (You should have about ½ cup of seeds.)

2. In a separate mixing bowl, whisk the raspberry vinegar and dry mustard together. Continue whisking and add the olive and vegetable oils in a steady stream.

3. Stir in ¼ cup of the reserved pomegranate seeds, the shallot, and chives. Season with salt and pepper. Cover and refrigerate until ready to use.

For the Lemon Cream

1. In a small mixing bowl, combine the crème fraîche, heavy cream, and lemon juice.

2. Season with salt, white pepper, and sugar. The lemon cream may be prepared ahead of time and stored in the refrigerator overnight.

To Serve

1. In a large salad bowl, toss the endive spears with the pomegranate vinaigrette.

2. In the center of each of 6 salad plates, make a mound of the dressed endive.

3. Drizzle each salad with the lemon cream and sprinkle with chervil sprigs, chopped chives, and pomegranate seeds.

Asian-Inspired Chicken Salad with Virginia Peanuts

Whenever I have a night off, I seem to end up in a Vietnamese restaurant. The healthful combinations of raw and cooked ingredients and fragrant, spicy flavors in Vietnamese cuisine are the inspiration for this refreshing, easy-to-make chicken salad. This stylish and exotic make-ahead dish is a showstopper for a warm-weather lunch and makes a charming addition to a picnic when packed into Chinese to-go containers.

&

Serves 6

6 cups well-seasoned chicken stock

6 boneless, skinless chicken breasts

2 cups finely julienned carrot

1 cup finely julienned celery

¼ cup thinly sliced red onion

½ cup julienned daikon radish

¼ cup cilantro leaves

3 tablespoons fresh lime juice

1 cup Clear Fish Sauce with Lime and Cilantro (see page 212)

¾ cup salted peanuts

18 leaves Boston lettuce

1. In a 4-quart saucepan, bring the chicken stock to a simmer and add the chicken. Gently poach the chicken for 12 minutes, or until the breasts are just cooked through. Using a slotted spoon, lift the chicken breasts out of the stock and let them cool on a plate. (Reserve the stock for another use.)

2. In a large mixing bowl, toss the carrot, celery, red onion, daikon radish, cilantro leaves, lime juice, Clear Fish Sauce with Lime and Cilantro, and ½ cup of the peanuts.

3. When the chicken is cool enough to handle, cut it into very thin strips and toss it with the vegetable mixture. The dish may be made in advance to this point and stored in the refrigerator overnight until ready to serve.

4. On each of 6 serving plates, form a cup with 3 lettuce leaves. Fill each lettuce cup with chicken salad and garnish with the remaining peanuts.

Cucumber Sorbet

Our guests find this simple Cucumber Sorbet tantalizing. It offers another dimension to the usual palate refresher. The unexpected accompaniment of cucumber salsa, featuring jalapeño peppers and fresh dill, teases the tongue. The coarse texture of the salsa accentuates the creamy, smooth consistency of the sorbet, while the contrast of iciness and subtle heat from the peppers plays a trick on the senses.

ও

Makes about 2 cups of salsa and 1½ quarts of sorbet

Cucumber Salsa

½ large European seedless cucumber, peeled and finely diced

1½ tablespoons finely chopped fresh dill

2 teaspoons finely diced jalapeño pepper

1 tablespoon finely diced red onion

2 tablespoons rice wine vinegar

Pinch of salt and sugar to taste

Cucumber Sorbet

2½ large European seedless cucumbers (not peeled)

¾ cup light corn syrup

½ cup sugar

½ cup lemon juice

1 teaspoon salt

¼ cup fresh dill

2 tablespoons citron-flavored vodka

2 egg whites

For the Cucumber Salsa

In a mixing bowl, combine the ingredients. Refrigerate until ready to use.

For the Cucumber Sorbet

1. Using a blender or food processor, puree the cucumbers (you should have about 4 cups). Strain through a fine mesh sieve.

2. Add the corn syrup, sugar, lemon juice, salt, dill, and vodka to the cucumber puree.

3. Whisk the egg whites until frothy and stir them into the cucumber mixture.

4. Freeze in an ice cream machine according to the manufacturer's instructions.

5. Serve the sorbet sprinkled with the cucumber salsa.

Lemon Verbena Sorbet

We often use this wonderfully refreshing sorbet as a palette cleanser before the meat course on our tasting menu. The lemon verbena tingles the taste buds and stimulates the appetite. As a dessert, the sorbet can be served with a splash of Limoncello — an Italian lemon liquor.

For the Lemon Verbena Sorbet

1. Combine the water and sugar in a heavy-bottomed saucepan over medium heat. Stir until the sugar is completely dissolved and the liquid is clear. Remove from heat.

2. Add the lemon verbena and let it steep for 1 hour.

3. Cool and strain through a fine mesh sieve.

4. Whisk in the lemon juice and egg white.

5. Freeze in an ice cream machine according to the manufacturer's instructions.

To make the Limoncello

1. Cut the lemons into four wedges and, using a tablespoon, scoop the fruit out of the rinds. (Save fruit for another use.) With a knife, carefully remove the white pith and discard it.

2. Combine the lemon rinds with the grain alcohol and allow it to macerate for 5 days.

3. Strain the liquor and combine it with the Simple Syrup.

4. Store the Limoncello in a covered bottle at room temperature.

Makes 2 quarts

Lemon Verbena Sorbet

1 quart water

4 cups sugar

8 ounces fresh lemon verbena

2 cups fresh lemon juice, strained

1 egg white, lightly beaten

Limoncello

5 lemons

½ liter grain alcohol

1 quart Simple Syrup (see page 218)

Main Dishes

છ૭

Wild Mushroom Napoleons

These crisp, savory napoleons are composed of layers of buttered phyllo, sprinkled with cheese and fresh herbs, cut into squares, and baked. Each layer is filled with a mixture of sautéed wild mushrooms, dressed with Sherry Vinaigrette, and tossed with a bit of frisée. A warm froth of buttery mushroom essence completes the dish.

৪০

Serves 6

Phyllo Crisps

¼ cup freshly grated Parmesan cheese

½ teaspoon chopped fresh thyme

½ teaspoon chopped fresh parsley

½ teaspoon chopped fresh rosemary

3 sheets phyllo dough

¼ cup clarified butter

Mushroom Sauce

1 pound white button mushrooms, wiped clean with a damp towel and roughly chopped

6 tablespoons cold butter

½ cup water

Salt to taste

To Make the Phyllo Crisps

1. Preheat the oven to 375 degrees. Line a baking sheet with parchment paper.

2. In a small bowl, stir the Parmesan and chopped herbs together.

3. On a cutting board, lay out one sheet of phyllo dough, brush with clarified butter, and sprinkle half the Parmesan cheese and herb mixture evenly on top. (Keep the remaining phyllo covered with a moistened tea towel.)

4. Place a second piece of phyllo on top of the seasoned phyllo sheet, brush with clarified butter, and sprinkle with the remaining cheese and herbs. Place a third sheet of phyllo on top and brush it with clarified butter.

5. Chill the layered phyllo in the refrigerator until the butter is firm, about 10 minutes.

6. Using a sharp knife, cut the buttered phyllo into 3 x 3-inch squares. Place the phyllo squares on the prepared baking sheet. Bake until golden brown (approximately 10 to 12 minutes).

7. Remove from the oven and cool. Store in an airtight container at room temperature until ready to serve.

For the Mushroom Sauce

1. Place the mushrooms in the bowl of a food processor and pulse until finely chopped.

2. In a large saucepan, melt 2 tablespoons of the butter over medium heat. Add the mushrooms and sauté for a minute. Add the water and bring the mushrooms to a boil. Cover the pan, remove from heat, and let steep for 15 minutes.

3. Strain the mushroom broth through a fine mesh sieve, pressing hard on the solids to extract as much flavor as possible. The mushroom broth may be refrigerated at this stage and rewarmed before serving.

4. Just before serving bring the broth to a boil in a medium saucepan. Reduce heat to a simmer and whisk in the remaining cold butter, 1 tablespoon at a time. Salt to taste.

5. If desired, buzz the sauce with a handheld blender to create a cappuccino-like froth.

Continued on page 132

To Serve

½ cup olive oil

1½ pounds assorted wild mushrooms
(such as shiitakes, chanterelles,
morels, or oyster mushrooms),
cut into bite-size pieces

2 tablespoons chopped shallot

1 teaspoon chopped garlic

Salt and freshly ground black pepper
to taste

¼ cup Sherry Vinaigrette
(see page 218)

1 head of frisée

6 sprigs fresh parsley

To Serve

1. In a large sauté pan, heat the olive oil over high heat. Add the wild mushrooms, lower the heat to medium, and sauté for 2 minutes. Add the shallot and garlic, season with salt and pepper, and cook for 3 more minutes, or until the mushrooms are lightly browned and the shallots are translucent.

2. Place the warm sautéed mushrooms in a mixing bowl and toss them with half of the Sherry Vinaigrette. In another mixing bowl, toss the frisée with the remaining vinaigrette.

3. Place ¼ cup of the mushroom mixture in the center of each warmed serving plate, sprinkle with the dressed frisée, and cover with a phyllo crisp. Place another ¼ cup of the mushroom mixture on top of the phyllo crisp and cover with a second crisp. Place another ¼ cup of the mushroom mixture on top.

4. Spoon the mushroom sauce around the plate and garnish with the remaining frisée and parsley.

Sesame-Crusted Sea Bass in an Aromatic Broth

Sesame seeds add an interesting textural component to this meltingly tender, sweet white fish. A flavorful broth accented with soy and honey provides an unexpected and lighter alternative to a predictable sauce. Steamed rice is a welcome accompaniment.

છ૭

For the Aromatic Broth

1. In a 2-quart saucepan, melt 1 tablespoon of the butter over medium heat. Add the mushrooms and cook until they soften.

2. Add the vermouth or wine and cook until it has almost completely evaporated. Add the stock, soy sauce, and honey, and simmer for 10 minutes.

3. Whisk in the remaining butter. Strain through a fine mesh sieve. The sauce may be made several hours in advance, held at room temperature, and re-warmed before serving.

For the Sea Bass

1. Season the sea bass with salt and pepper, and dip both sides in the sesame seeds.

2. In a large skillet, heat 2 tablespoons of the butter over medium heat. Cook the fillets until they are golden brown on both sides and just cooked through. (If the sesame seeds start to pop, the pan is too hot.)

3. In a medium saucepan, warm the broth over low heat. Add the shrimp, mushrooms, and preserved lemon. Simmer until the shrimp are just cooked, about 2 minutes. Remove the pan from the heat and add the tomatoes.

4. Place 1 fish fillet in the center of each of 6 soup plates and garnish with the shrimp, mushrooms, and tomatoes. Ladle the sauce into the bowl and serve.

Serves 6

Aromatic Broth

4 tablespoons (½ stick) unsalted butter

2 cups finely chopped white button mushrooms

½ cup dry vermouth or dry white wine

2 cups chicken or Vegetable Stock (see page 221)

½ cup soy sauce

⅓ cup honey

Sea Bass

6 fillets sea bass, about 4 ounces each

Salt and freshly ground white pepper to taste

½ cup sesame seeds

3 tablespoons clarified butter

9 raw shrimp, peeled, deveined, and split in half lengthwise

1 cup small white button mushrooms, quartered

2 tablespoons finely diced preserved lemon (found in gourmet stores)

9 grape or cherry tomatoes, cut in half

Crispy Seared Rockfish on Braised Baby Bok Choy with Sweet-and-Sour Fish Sauce

You'll love the flavor, succulence, and versatility of braised bok choy. In this dish, we rest a fillet of seared, golden fish on a bed of bok choy and drizzle the plate with our version of an Asian sweet-and-sour sauce.

We serve this light, healthful Asian-inspired dish as a first course, but it works equally well as a main course. The sauce can be made in advance and combines well with almost any seafood or poultry.

ജ

Serves 6

Braised Baby Bok Choy

3 whole baby bok choy, split in half lengthwise

2 tablespoons clarified butter

¼ cup white wine

¼ cup Vegetable Stock (see page 221) or water

3 tablespoons whole butter

Salt and freshly ground black pepper to taste

Crispy Seared Rockfish

6 skinless fillets of rockfish or striped bass, about 3 ounces each

Salt and freshly ground black pepper to taste

4 tablespoons clarified butter

To Serve

1 recipe Sweet-and-Sour Fish Sauce (see page 220)

Pickled ginger (for garnish)

For the Braised Baby Bok Choy

1. Bring a large pot of salted water to a boil. Cook the bok choy in the boiling water for 2 to 3 minutes, or until the core is tender. Using a slotted spoon, remove the bok choy from the water and drain well on paper towels.

2. In a large skillet, heat the clarified butter over high heat until it is almost smoking. Carefully place the drained bok choy, cut side down, in the skillet and cook for about 2 minutes, or until it is golden brown.

3. Deglaze the pan with the white wine and reduce by half.

4. Add the Vegetable Stock or water and reduce by half.

5. Carefully whisk in the whole butter.

6. Season with salt and pepper to taste. Keep warm while you cook the fish.

For the Crispy Seared Rockfish

1. Season the fish fillets with salt and pepper.

2. In a 10-inch nonstick skillet, heat the clarified butter over high heat until almost smoking. Place the fillets in the skillet, turn the heat to medium, and cook for about 2 minutes until crispy and golden brown.

3. Flip the fish onto the other side and cook for another 30 seconds, or until the fish is just cooked through.

4. Remove the fish from the pan and keep warm.

To Serve

1. Place a piece of bok choy on each of 6 warmed plates and lay a fish fillet on each one.

2. Drizzle the warm Sweet-and-Sour Fish Sauce around the fish in small pools. Garnish with pickled ginger.

Medallions of Poached Salmon on Spinach-Filled Tortelli

This is a delicate, light, and totally irresistible way to serve fresh salmon. The fillets are cut into small medallions, briefly poached, and placed on buttery spinach-filled pasta pillows nested on bouquets of emerald-green watercress. A splash of radiant yellow butter sauce adds a final dazzling flourish. The vibrant colors and seductive textures of the dish are enough to make salmon seem sexy again.

૪૭

Serves 6

Spinach and Cottage Cheese Filling

½ pound cottage cheese

2 tablespoons olive oil

2 whole garlic cloves, peeled and lightly crushed

2 pounds fresh spinach leaves, stemmed and washed

½ cup freshly grated Parmesan cheese

1 egg

Salt and freshly ground black pepper to taste

Freshly grated nutmeg to taste

Spinach and Cottage Cheese Tortelli

1 recipe Pasta Dough (see page 214)

¼ cup flour (for dusting)

2 tablespoons yellow cornmeal

Butter Sauce

1 cup chicken or Vegetable Stock (see page 221)

½ pound cold, unsalted butter, cut into cubes

Salt and freshly ground white pepper to taste

Salmon and Tortelli

3 pounds boneless, skinless fresh salmon fillet

Salt and freshly ground white pepper to taste

1 tablespoon vegetable oil

1 cup chopped carrot

1 cup chopped onion

For the Spinach and Cottage Cheese Filling

1. Place the cottage cheese in a sieve and drain for a few minutes to let the excess liquid (whey) run off.

2. In a large sauté pan (or in two smaller pans), heat the olive oil over medium heat. Add the whole garlic cloves and sauté until just beginning to brown. Remove the garlic. Quickly add the spinach and toss with tongs until it is just wilted. Let cool, drain thoroughly, and finely chop the cooked spinach.

3. Place the spinach in a mixing bowl and stir in the drained cottage cheese, Parmesan, egg, salt, pepper, and nutmeg.

For the Spinach and Cottage Cheese Tortelli

1. Using a pasta machine, roll the pasta dough out into very thin sheets.

2. Dust a work surface with flour and lay out the sheets of pasta on the floured surface.

3. Using a 4-inch round, fluted cookie cutter, cut out 12 rounds of dough.

4. Place 3 tablespoons of the spinach and cottage cheese filling in the center of each dough round and, using your finger, moisten the edges of the dough with water. Fold the dough in half around the filling and press the edges firmly to seal. Wrap the stuffed pasta around your finger and pinch the ends together to form each tortelli. Dust a baking sheet with the cornmeal and lay the tortelli out on it. Refrigerate until ready to cook.

For the Butter Sauce

1. In a small saucepan, reduce the stock by half over medium heat.

2. Reduce the heat to low and, piece by piece, whisk in the butter. Season with salt and white pepper to taste. Keep warm.

For the Salmon and Tortelli

1. Using a 2-inch round cookie cutter, stamp out 12 medallions of salmon, approximately 1 inch thick. Season with salt and pepper.

2. In a large soup pot, heat the oil over medium heat. Add the carrot, onion, and celery and cook until the vegetables begin to soften, about 5 minutes.

3. Add the white wine, peppercorns, and herbs, and cook until the wine has almost completely evaporated.

4. Add the stock, lemon juice, and salt, and bring to a simmer.

Continued on page 138

1 cup chopped celery

1 cup white wine

1 tablespoon whole black peppercorns

2 sprigs fresh thyme

4 sprigs fresh parsley

2 quarts of chicken stock or water

Juice of 1 lemon

1 tablespoon salt

1 recipe spinach and cottage cheese tortelli

Garnishes

1 bunch watercress, large stems removed

¼ cup chopped fresh tomatoes

5. Place the salmon medallions in a strainer or colander, small enough to be lowered into the pot, and completely submerge the salmon medallions into the simmering liquid. Poach the fillets in the liquid for 4 minutes or until they are just barely cooked through.

6. Lift the fillets out of the liquid and keep warm.

7. Meanwhile, bring a large pot of salted water to a boil.

8. Add the tortelli to the boiling water and cook for 1½ minutes. Drain.

To Serve

1. Place a few sprigs of watercress in each of 6 soup plates. Place 2 tortelli on top of the watercress and a medallion of salmon on each tortelli. Garnish the salmon with chopped tomatoes.

2. Splash the butter sauce around the plate.

Spruced-Up Turkey

These days, commercial turkeys and chickens too often lack flavor and succulence. Here is a way to make your Thanksgiving turkey or a simple roast chicken taste like those your grandmother might have raised on the farm. The spruce branches (taken from an ornamental blue spruce, or Norway spruce) impart a delightfully wild and woodsy taste. Soaking the turkey overnight in a brine solution infuses the meat with exotic, fragrant flavors and plumps the bird. Don't feel obligated to include every single one of the ingredients for the brine if any are too difficult to obtain. Rather, use the list of ingredients as a guideline and improvise as you wish.

For the Brine

1. Combine all ingredients except the boiling water in a 5-gallon heat-proof container large enough to hold the turkey.
2. Pour the boiling water over the brine ingredients and let the mixture cool to room temperature.
3. Submerge the turkey in the brine, cover, and refrigerate overnight.

For the Turkey

1. Preheat the oven to 325 degrees.
2. Remove the turkey from the brine and rinse it off under cold water.
3. Place the turkey in a roasting pan. Carefully dip the cheesecloth into the melted butter and lay it on top of the turkey.
4. Place the turkey in the oven and roast for 3 to 4 hours, basting the cheesecloth with melted butter about every 30 minutes. The turkey is done when a thermometer inserted into the thickest part of the thigh registers 160 degrees.
5. Remove the turkey from the oven and allow it to rest for 30 minutes. Carefully remove the cheesecloth and place the turkey on a serving platter. Surround the platter with the spruce branches.

Serves 12 to 14

Brine

1¼ cups kosher salt

3¼ cups sugar

2 cups honey

2 lemons, cut in half

6 sprigs fresh parsley

6 sprigs fresh dill

6 sprigs fresh thyme

6 sprigs fresh tarragon

6 sprigs fresh sage

2 sprigs fresh rosemary

2 tablespoons mustard seeds

2 tablespoons fennel seeds

2 whole cinnamon sticks

5 whole bay leaves

8 whole cloves

1 tablespoon juniper berries

1 tablespoon whole cardamom pods

2 tablespoons whole black peppercorns

5 whole star anise

1 tablespoon whole allspice

1 two-foot-long spruce branch, washed and cut into small pieces

1 one-foot-long piece of sassafras root, washed and cut into small pieces (If you can't find whole sassafras root, 3 to 4 ounces of loose sassafras tea can be substituted.)

2 gallons boiling water

Turkey

1 fresh turkey, about 18 to 20 pounds

1 2 x 2-foot square of cheesecloth

2 pounds (eight sticks) butter, melted and warm

Spruce branches (for garnish)

Bay Scallops with Mushrooms, Peppers, and Grilled Italian Sausage

I've always loved the lusty combination of scallops, peppers, and Italian sausage. In this dish we use tiny, succulent Nantucket Bay scallops and sometimes present them as a first course served in a scallop shell. If bay scallops are unobtainable, larger sea scallops may be substituted.

In order for the scallops to turn a lovely golden-brown color, it is essential that they be thoroughly dried before you attempt to sauté them. A spritz of Pernod just before serving perfumes the scallops with the fragrance of fennel.

&

1. Pour a few drops of vegetable oil into a small sauté pan, add the sausages, and cook over medium heat until they are lightly browned and cooked through. Drain the sausages on paper towels. Set aside and keep warm.

2. In a large sauté pan, heat half of the vegetable oil over high heat. Add the peppers and mushrooms. Sauté quickly for several minutes. Add ½ tablespoon of garlic and sauté for 1 more minute. Remove from the pan and keep warm.

3. Slice each sausage on the bias into ½-inch slices.

4. In the same pan, add the remaining vegetable oil over high heat. Sauté the scallops for several minutes until just lightly browned. Do not overcook. Add the remaining garlic and the peppers and mushrooms, and continue cooking for a few more minutes.

5. Add the lemon juice, remove from heat, and swirl in the butter and parsley. Add the sausage slices.

To Serve

1. Divide the scallop mixture among 6 serving plates and sprinkle the scallops with a few drops of Pernod.

2. Pool the Red Pepper Coulis around each of the plates and serve.

Serves 6

¼ cup plus a few drops vegetable oil

3 sweet Italian sausages

2 red bell peppers, seeded and cut into 1-inch cubes

2 green bell peppers, seeded and cut into 1-inch cubes

18 white button mushrooms, quartered

1 tablespoon minced garlic

2 pounds fresh bay scallops

Juice of 1 lemon

3 tablespoons butter

1 tablespoon chopped fresh parsley

To Serve

2 tablespoons Pernod

1 cup Red Pepper Coulis (see page 216)

Eggplant Ravioli with Medallions of Maine Lobster and Tomato-Basil Butter

Who, in this day and age, would want to make homemade ravioli? you might ask. Instead of a trip to a day spa, you could embark on the job of rolling, filling, and cutting these "little pillows" with the mind-set that this is not work but rather a therapeutic process designed to be calming, centering, and deeply sensual. Think of the money you could save by healing yourself at home in the privacy of your own kitchen.

This recipe originated in our kitchen (without the lobster) as a vegetarian dish. One day we added the lobster meat and found the combination of flavors titillating. The dish soon became our most popular first course. Fortunately, the ravioli and the tomato-basil butter sauce can be fully prepared a day in advance.

જી

Serves 8

Eggplant Filling

1 large eggplant, peeled and halved

1 teaspoon kosher salt

Nonstick cooking spray

2 tablespoons unsalted butter

½ cup diced onion

⅓ cup diced tomato, canned or fresh

1 teaspoon chopped fresh thyme

½ teaspoon Roasted Garlic
(see page 217)

1 tablespoon pine nuts, toasted

⅓ cup mascarpone cheese

1 tablespoon freshly grated Parmesan cheese

Salt and freshly ground black pepper to taste

¼ teaspoon sugar

Eggplant Ravioli

½ recipe Pasta Dough
(see page 214)

2 tablespoons yellow cornmeal

Tomato-Basil Butter

2 tablespoons unsalted butter

½ cup roughly chopped onion

¼ cup roughly chopped carrot

¼ cup roughly chopped celery

1½ cups diced fresh or canned tomatoes

For the Eggplant Filling

1. Place the eggplant in a colander, sprinkle it with kosher salt, allow it to drain for 1 hour, and rinse with cold water.

2. Preheat the oven to 350 degrees.

3. Spray a baking sheet with nonstick cooking spray. Place the eggplant, cut side down, on the baking sheet and bake for about 1 hour.

4. In a medium-size skillet, melt the butter over medium heat. Add the onion and cook for about 5 minutes, until it's translucent. Add the diced tomato, thyme, and Roasted Garlic, and cook for 5 minutes more.

5. Remove the eggplant from the oven, cool, and roughly chop.

6. In a blender or food processor, puree the tomato mixture with the eggplant until smooth, then add the pine nuts, cheeses, salt, pepper, and sugar, and process until the mixture is smooth.

For the Eggplant Ravioli

1. Using a pasta machine, roll the pasta dough out into very thin sheets.

2. Dust a work surface with flour and lay out the sheets of pasta on the floured surface.

3. Using a 2½-inch round, fluted cookie cutter, cut out 48 rounds of dough.

4. Place one teaspoon of the eggplant filling in the center of each dough round and, using your finger, moisten the edges of the dough with water. Fold the dough in half around the filling and press the edges firmly to seal each ravioli.

5. Dust a baking sheet with cornmeal and lay the ravioli out on it. Refrigerate until ready to cook.

For the Tomato-Basil Butter

1. In a 4-quart saucepan, melt the butter over low heat. Add the onion, carrot, and celery, and cook until the onion is translucent.

2. Add the tomatoes, Vegetable Stock or water, parsley, bay leaf, thyme, basil, sugar, salt, and pepper. Simmer for 20 to 30 minutes until the vegetables are completely tender.

3. In a blender or food processor, puree the mixture until smooth. Strain through a fine mesh sieve.

4. Meanwhile, in a 2-quart saucepan, bring the cream to a boil, immediately reduce the heat, and simmer until the cream has reduced to 1 cup.

5. Combine the reduced cream and the pureed tomato mixture. Correct the seasoning, if necessary, and set aside until ready to serve.

To Serve

1. Bring a large pot of salted water to a boil.

2. Add the ravioli to the boiling water and cook for 1½ minutes. Drain the ravioli, place in a large mixing bowl, and toss it with the warm tomato-basil butter.

3. Meanwhile, melt the 2 tablespoons of butter in a sauté pan over medium heat. Add the lobster meat and thoroughly warm it in the melted butter.

4. Divide the ravioli and lobster among 8 warm serving bowls. Garnish with pine nuts, basil leaves, and a drizzle of olive oil.

1½ cups Vegetable Stock (see page 221) or water

1 teaspoon chopped fresh parsley

½ bay leaf

1 teaspoon fresh thyme leaves, or ½ teaspoon dried thyme

10 leaves fresh basil

1 teaspoon sugar

Salt and freshly ground black pepper to taste

2 cups heavy cream

To Serve

2 tablespoons butter

1 pound cooked lobster meat, cut into 1-inch pieces

2 tablespoons toasted pine nuts

Basil leaves (for garnish)

2 tablespoons olive oil

Chicken and Dumplings

Chicken and dumplings was a Southern noonday "dinner" that was meant to provide enough nourishment for the farm laborers to work in 'dem fields 'til the cows came home. Recently, I felt an irresistible urge to resurrect and lighten this dish. We offer it in miniature porcelain casseroles as a soulful appetizer that provides a little cushion in the stomach before a multicourse meal. It's also welcome as a main course or buffet dish.

In this recipe the sauce is not thickened with a flour-based roux; instead, both the chicken stock and the cream are reduced separately before combining them, giving the sauce a rich, savory flavor and a satiny texture. When fresh morels are in season, they make a luxurious addition; however, white button mushrooms will work as well. While this dish may be a cosmopolitan cousin of its namesake, after a few forkfuls your guests just might be whistlin' Dixie.

For the Dumpling Dough

1. In a small saucepan, heat the milk and butter until the butter is melted. Remove from heat.

2. In a mixing bowl, combine the flour, baking powder, and salt. Stir in the club soda and the milk-butter mixture until the dough forms a ball. (Take care not to overwork the dough, or the dumplings may become tough.)

3. Cover and let stand at room temperature for 30 minutes.

For the Chicken and Dumplings

1. In a 4-quart saucepan, bring the chicken stock to a simmer. Add the chicken, carrots, and thyme. Poach the chicken and carrots for 12 minutes, or until the chicken is just cooked through and the carrots are tender. Using a slotted spoon, lift the chicken and carrots out of the stock and let them cool on a plate. Boil the chicken stock until it is reduced by half.

2. In a small saucepan, reduce the cream by half. Slowly whisk the reduced cream into the reduced chicken stock. Season with salt and pepper and set the sauce aside.

3. Cut the chicken into bite-size pieces.

4. Heat the butter in a small skillet over medium-high heat. Add the morels or button mushrooms, season with salt and pepper, and sauté for 2 minutes.

5. Stir the chicken, carrots, and mushrooms into the sauce.

6. Drop the dumpling dough by teaspoonfuls into the simmering sauce, cover tightly, and simmer for 7 minutes.

7. Serve the chicken and dumplings in a deep-dish platter or soup tureen.

Serves 6

Dumpling Dough

¾ cup milk

3 tablespoons butter

2 cups all-purpose flour

1 tablespoon baking powder

¾ teaspoon salt

¼ cup club soda

Chicken and Dumplings

4 cups chicken stock

3 boneless, skinless chicken breasts

½ cup diced carrots

1 sprig fresh thyme

1½ cups heavy cream

Salt and freshly ground black pepper to taste

2 tablespoons butter

1 cup chopped morel or white button mushrooms

Braised Duck Legs on Wilted Watercress in an Aromatic Asian Broth

Home cooks are sometimes reluctant to prepare duck. Roasting a duck is difficult because the breast is often overcooked by the time the legs are tender. Carving a duck can also be daunting. Ideally, the leg and breast should be prepared separately.

This dish utilizes only the legs — the meat that is richest in flavor. You may be able to buy duck legs separately. If not, purchase whole ducks and remove the legs from the carcass. (The breasts may be roasted on the carcass or removed from the bone and seared in a pan for another meal.)

The duck legs are rolled in an aromatic spice mixture, seared, and braised. The tender, fragrant meat slips off the bone easily and is mounded on a nest of watercress, capped with an optional accompaniment of seared foie gras, and presented in a flavorful, clear broth. A bit of candied orange zest and sections of fresh orange echo the classic duck à l'orange but with a whole new attitude.

Chicken legs and thighs may be substituted for the duck if you wish.

Serves 8

Duck Spice Mix

I tablespoon star anise

I tablespoon whole cardamom

I tablespoon whole cloves

¼ cup white peppercorns

4 cinnamon sticks, about 3 inches each

¼ cup coriander seeds

¼ cup whole cumin

¼ cup fennel seeds

Duck Legs

4 duck legs

Salt and freshly ground black pepper to taste

I recipe duck spice mix

⅓ cup grape-seed or vegetable oil

I strip smoked bacon, chopped

I carrot, chopped roughly

I onion, chopped roughly

I stalk celery, chopped roughly

¼ cup tomato paste

½ cup red wine

6 cups chicken stock

For the Duck Spice Mix

Combine the spices in a spice grinder and grind them into a fine powder.

For the Duck Legs

1. Preheat the oven to 400 degrees.

2. Season the duck legs with salt and black pepper. On the skin side only, generously season the duck legs with the duck spice.

3. In a small roasting pan, heat the oil over high heat. Sear the duck legs, skin side down, until golden brown. Turn the legs over and sear the other side for 2 to 3 minutes, until browned. Remove the legs from the roasting pan and set aside.

4. Reduce the heat to medium and add the bacon. Cook for 4 minutes, stirring with a wooden spoon. Add the carrots, onions, and celery and cook for 5 minutes more.

5. Add the tomato paste and stir until the vegetables are evenly coated. Continue to cook, stirring, for about 3 minutes, or until tomato paste starts to brown on the bottom of the pan. Deglaze with red wine and simmer until the wine has almost evaporated.

6. Add the stock and season with salt and pepper. Return the reserved legs to the pan, cover with foil, and place in the oven for 2 hours, or until the meat is tender and pulls away from the bone. Remove the pan from the oven and allow the duck legs to cool in the liquid.

7. Once the duck legs have cooled, take them out of the liquid. Remove and discard all bones and skin. Store the meat in the refrigerator until ready to serve. Strain the liquid and refrigerate until ready to serve. The recipe may be prepared to this point one day in advance.

Continued on page 148

Candied Orange Zest Garnish

2 oranges

2 cups water

¾ cup sugar

Garnishes

1 fresh foie gras, about 1¼ pounds
   (optional)

Salt and freshly ground black pepper
   to taste

1 recipe Wilted Watercress
   (see page 169)

2 oranges (reserved from candied
   orange zest garnish), peeled, pith
   removed, and carefully sectioned

To Make the Candied Orange Zest Garnish

1. Remove the orange part of the skin in long strips with a vegetable peeler.

2. Using a sharp knife, julienne the zest into fine slivers. (Reserve the zested oranges for garnishing the dish.)

3. In a small saucepan, combine the water and sugar and bring to a boil. Add the julienned zest and cook over low heat for about 20 minutes. The zest can be prepared up to 3 days in advance and stored in its syrup. (Drain before using.)

To Serve

1. In a medium saucepan, heat the duck meat in the broth over medium heat and keep warm.

2. Preheat a cast-iron skillet over high heat.

3. Soak the foie gras in a bowl of ice water for 10 minutes to draw out the blood and firm up the flesh. Separate the two lobes of the liver, removing any fat or sinew. Using a very sharp knife dipped in warm water, slice the liver on the bias into ¼-inch slices. Season with salt and pepper.

4. Sear the foie gras in the hot skillet for about 30 seconds on each side, or just until a rich, brown crust forms. Remove from the skillet and blot on paper towels.

5. Place a small mound of Wilted Watercress in the center of each of 8 warm serving bowls. Place the duck meat on top of the watercress and a piece of foie gras on top of the duck meat.

6. Ladle the broth around the duck. Garnish each bowl with orange sections and candied orange zest.

Veal Medallions with Country Ham Ravioli

Veal and ham have long been a classic combination, as in saltimbocca à la Romana (veal scaloppine with ham and sage). In this version, our famous Virginia country ham is combined with Fontina and Parmesan cheeses to form a seductive ravioli filling. The veal tenderloins are pan roasted, sliced, and interspersed with the plump, savory ravioli, which mimic the sensual texture of the veal. A reduction of veal stock, ham, and sage leaves brings all of the elements together in a concentrated and robust sauce.

I recommend making the ravioli and the sauce a day in advance.

Serves 6

Ravioli Filling

1 tablespoon butter

1 tablespoon minced shallot

¼ cup balsamic vinegar

1 cup heavy cream

2 tablespoons freshly grated Parmesan cheese

2 cups freshly grated Fontina cheese

Salt and freshly ground black pepper to taste

Country Ham Ravioli

½ recipe Pasta Dough (see page 214)

¼ cup flour

½ cup thinly sliced and diced country ham

2 tablespoons yellow cornmeal

Sauce

2 cups rich veal stock

1 slice country ham, chopped

2 sprigs fresh thyme

4 sage leaves

Salt and freshly ground black pepper to taste

Veal Medallions

3 boneless veal butt tenderloins, trimmed (about 1 pound each)

Salt and freshly ground black pepper to taste

2 tablespoons olive oil

For the Ravioli Filling

1. In a small saucepan, melt the butter over medium heat and cook the shallot until translucent.

2. Pour the vinegar over the shallots and continue cooking until the vinegar is reduced and becomes syrupy.

3. Whisk in the cream and simmer. Gradually whisk in the Parmesan and Fontina cheeses. Season with salt and pepper.

4. Pour the mixture into a plastic container and refrigerate until well chilled.

For the Country Ham Ravioli

1. Using a pasta machine, roll the pasta dough out into very thin sheets.

2. Dust a work surface with the flour and lay out the sheets of pasta on the floured surface.

3. Using a 2½-inch round, fluted cookie cutter, cut out 36 rounds of dough.

4. Place one teaspoon of the filling and one teaspoon of country ham in the center of each dough round. Using your finger, moisten the edges of the dough with water. Cover with another disk of pasta dough and press the edges firmly to seal each ravioli. Dust a baking sheet with cornmeal and lay the ravioli out on it. Refrigerate until ready to cook. The ravioli can be made a day in advance.

For the Sauce

1. In a 2-quart saucepan, simmer the veal stock for 20 minutes, or until reduced by half.

2. Add the ham, thyme, and sage and simmer for another 5 minutes.

3. Cover and remove from heat. Let steep for 10 to 15 minutes. Strain the sauce and season with a pinch of salt and pepper. The sauce may be made in advance and stored in the refrigerator for several days.

For the Veal Medallions

1. Season the tenderloins with salt and pepper.

2. In a large skillet, heat the olive oil over high heat. Sear the veal on both sides until well browned.

3. Reduce the heat and continue cooking until the meat is cooked through but still a bit pink in the center. Keep warm in a 200-degree oven.

For the Mushroom Garnish

1. In a large skillet, heat the olive oil over high heat. Add the mushrooms and sauté until lightly browned, about 1 minute.

2. Add the shallot, garlic, salt, and pepper and cook for 2 minutes more. Keep warm in a 200-degree oven.

To Serve

1. Bring the veal sauce to a gentle simmer.

2. Bring a large pot of salted water to a boil. Add the ravioli to the boiling water and cook for 1½ minutes (just until al dente). Drain the ravioli, place them in a large mixing bowl, and toss with a little warm veal sauce.

3. Meanwhile, slice the tenderloins into ¾-inch medallions.

4. Intersperse the veal slices and ravioli on each of 6 warmed serving plates. Sprinkle a few of the mushrooms on the plates and surround with the veal sauce.

Mushroom Garnish

2 tablespoons olive oil

2 cups assorted fresh, wild mushrooms (such as chanterelles, oysters, and morels), quartered, stems removed

1 teaspoon minced shallot

½ teaspoon minced garlic

Salt and freshly ground black pepper to taste

Boneless Rack of Lamb with Minted Tomato and Cucumber Relish

In the summer, when the garden is full of tomatoes, cucumbers, and fresh herbs, I love making this vinegary, spicy minted tomato and cucumber relish to offset the richness of grilled lamb. The bold flavors of mint, cumin, and dill perfume these simple, everyday vegetables, transforming them into an exotic and refreshing accompaniment — more healthful and satisfying than a rich, time-consuming sauce. (A leg of lamb will also lend itself to this preparation.)

෨

Serves 6

Minted Tomato and Cucumber Relish

4 tablespoons cooked chickpeas

1 small red onion, diced

1 English cucumber, diced

3 tomatoes, seeded and diced

2 tablespoons chopped fresh mint leaves

1 tablespoon chopped fresh dill

2 tablespoons rice wine vinegar

1 teaspoon crushed red pepper flakes

1½ teaspoons ground cumin

1 teaspoon minced garlic

1 teaspoon minced shallot

½ teaspoon grated lemon zest

3 tablespoons olive oil

Salt and freshly ground black pepper to taste

Lamb

3 racks of lamb, about 1¼ pounds each (Ask your butcher to remove the loins from the bone. The bones may be saved to make a lamb stock for another use.)

Salt and freshly ground black pepper to taste

Garnish

Shoestring Potatoes (see page 170)

For the Minted Tomato and Cucumber Relish

1. In a mixing bowl, combine the chickpeas, onion, cucumber, tomatoes, mint, and dill.

2. Using a wooden spoon, gently stir in the vinegar, red pepper flakes, cumin, garlic, shallot, lemon zest, and olive oil. Season with salt and pepper. Store in the refrigerator until ready to serve.

For the Lamb

1. Preheat the grill to high and preheat the oven to 400 degrees.

2. Season the lamb with salt and pepper.

3. Grill or broil the lamb enough to crisp and lightly char the exterior on all sides.

4. Place the lamb in a roasting pan and bake for about 14 to 15 minutes (for medium rare).

5. Remove the lamb, place it on a cutting board, and let it rest for 5 minutes. Slice each loin into 6 medallions.

To Serve

Serve the sliced lamb on a platter with the relish and Shoestring Potatoes.

Pistachio-Crusted Lamb Chops on Rutabaga Rösti with Gingered Carrot Sauce

These colorful and crunchy lamb chops are irresistible. The racks are roasted whole, and the meat is then removed from the bone, coated with a mustard and brown sugar glaze, rolled in chopped pistachios, and sliced into medallions.

The gingered carrot sauce has only three ingredients and couldn't be simpler. The sauce is so versatile it can even be used with fish dishes.

The addition of rutabaga to the accompanying rösti potato cake contributes an unexpected hint of natural sweetness that enhances both the carrot sauce and the flavor of the pistachios.

Serves 6

Gingered Carrot Sauce

1 quart organic carrot juice (available in health-food stores or the natural-food section of your supermarket)

1 one-inch chunk fresh ginger root, peeled

1½ cups crème fraîche

Salt and freshly ground white pepper to taste

Rutabaga Rösti

2 large Idaho baking potatoes

1 medium rutabaga, peeled and quartered

1 medium onion, finely chopped

Salt and freshly ground white pepper to taste

½ cup clarified butter

Lamb

3 one-and-a-half-pound racks of lamb, each comprising about 8 rib bones

Salt and freshly ground black pepper to taste

½ cup Dijon mustard

½ pound brown sugar

1 cup coarsely chopped pistachios

For the Gingered Carrot Sauce

1. Place the carrot juice and ginger root in a 2-quart saucepan and simmer over medium heat, whisking occasionally, until the carrot juice is reduced to 1 cup.

2. Remove and discard the ginger root and, over low heat, whisk in the crème fraîche. Season with salt and white pepper. The sauce may be made in advance, stored in the refrigerator, and rewarmed before serving.

For the Rutabaga Rösti

1. Peel the potatoes, leaving them whole. Combine with the rutabaga and steam for 15 minutes. Let cool.

2. Using the large holed blade of a box grater, shred the potatoes and rutabaga. Fold in the finely chopped onion.

3. Season the shredded vegetables with salt and pepper and form them into 6 cakes.

4. In a large skillet, heat half of the clarified butter over medium heat. Carefully place 3 cakes in the skillet and brown them on both sides for about 5 to 7 minutes per side. Remove and drain on paper towels. Repeat with the remaining clarified butter and vegetable cakes. The röstis can be made up to 1 hour in advance and rewarmed before serving.

For the Lamb

1. Preheat the oven to 400 degrees.

2. Season the lamb with salt and pepper.

3. Place the lamb in a roasting pan and bake for about 25 minutes.

4. Remove the lamb, place it on a cutting board, and let it rest for 5 minutes. Lay the blade of a sharp knife against the bone and slip the meat off 2 of the racks in one piece, leaving one rack as is.

5. Meanwhile, in a small mixing bowl, whisk the mustard and brown sugar together. Using a pastry brush, coat the meat with the mustard mixture, then roll each rack in the chopped pistachios. Return to the oven and bake for an additional 10 minutes. Remove the lamb from the oven and let rest

for 5 minutes. Slice each boneless loin into 6 medallions and carve the bone-in rack into 6 chops by cutting between the bones.

To Serve

1. Reheat the gingered carrot sauce and the rutabaga röstis.
2. Place a warm rösti in the center of each of 6 serving plates. Rest 2 of the boneless medallions and 1 bone-in chop against each rösti.
3. Dribble the gingered carrot sauce over each plate.

Surf and Turf: Tenderloin of Beef and Maine Lobster with Sweet Corn Sauté and Red Bell Pepper Coulis

Nothing tastes better during the height of summer than fresh sweet corn, Maine lobsters, and steaks on the grill. This dish combines all three in a version of surf and turf that actually makes sense. The corn's crisp, succulent texture complements both the lobster and the beef. The voluptuous buttery flavors of the corn sauté and the Red Pepper Coulis unify the dish. You can, of course, eliminate either the lobster or the beef if you wish and simply offer one or the other with the same accompaniments.

Begin by preparing the Red Pepper Coulis on page 216. Reserve and keep warm. The coulis may be made a day in advance and kept refrigerated until ready to serve.

ℰꙮ

Serves 6

Corn Sauté

6 ears fresh sweet corn (approximately 5 to 6 cups corn kernels)

4 strips bacon, diced

1 red bell pepper, finely diced

1 green bell pepper, finely diced

1 tablespoon white vinegar

1 tablespoon sugar

Salt and freshly ground black pepper to taste

1½ tablespoons chopped fresh cilantro

Lobster

3 live lobsters, about 1½ pounds each

¼ cup vegetable oil

¼ cup white wine

For the Corn Sauté

1. Shuck the corn, brushing off all the silk. Strip the kernels off the ears with a sharp knife.

2. In a 2-quart saucepan, place the bacon in a sauté pan and cook until crisp and brown.

3. Add the red and green bell peppers to the pan and sweat over medium heat for about 2 minutes. Add the corn and sauté for 3 to 4 minutes more.

4. Add the vinegar, sugar, salt, pepper, and cilantro.

5. Remove the corn mixture from the pan and keep warm until ready to serve. The corn sauté can be made one hour before serving and reheated.

To Cook the Lobster Claws

1. Hold the lobsters with a kitchen towel and carefully pull off the claws and tails. (Discard the bodies or keep them to flavor a lobster stock or soup.)

2. In a large kettle or steamer, bring 2 inches of salted water to a rolling boil. Add the claws, cover, and cook for 8 minutes.

3. Remove the claws from the steamer and plunge them into ice water to stop the cooking. Remove the claws from the ice water.

4. Using a mallet, crack the claws and knuckles and remove the meat. Reserve the claw and knuckle meat in the refrigerator until ready to use. This can be done a day in advance.

To Cook the Tails

1. Using a sharp knife, cut through the center of the shells, dividing the raw tails in half lengthwise. Leave the meat in the shells.

2. In a skillet, heat the vegetable oil over high heat until almost smoking. Add the lobster tails in their shells, cover, and cook for 3 minutes.

3. Add the white wine, cover, and cook for 1 minute more.

4. Remove the tail meat from the shells and keep warm.

Continued on page 158

Beef

6 beef tenderloin filets, about 4 ounces
    each

Salt and freshly ground black pepper
    to taste

6 pinches of sugar

To Serve and Garnish

I recipe Roasted Red Pepper
    (see page 217)

I recipe Red Pepper Coulis
    (see page 216)

I recipe Crispy Fried Onions
    (see page 213)

I bunch frisée or watercress

For the Beef

1. Season each filet of beef with salt and pepper and sprinkle with a pinch of
   sugar.

2. Preheat the grill to high heat.

3. Place each filet on the grill and cook until medium rare (about 2 to
   3 minutes on each side).

4. Remove the beef from the grill, cover with foil, and keep warm.

To Serve and Garnish

1. Coarsely chop the reserved lobster claws and knuckle meat and toss it with
   the corn sauté.

2. If necessary, reheat the lobster, beef, Roasted Red Pepper, corn sauté, and
   Red Pepper Coulis.

3. In the center of a large platter, mound the corn sauté.

4. Slice each filet of beef into three slices on the bias.

5. Alternate the slices of beef with the lobster tails and Roasted Red Pepper
   on top of the corn sauté.

6. Garnish the platter with Crispy Fried Onions and a bouquet of frisée or
   watercress. Drizzle the Red Pepper Coulis around the platter.

Scaloppine of Chicken with Grapefruit and Pink Peppercorns

This method of preparing chicken is fast, easy, and elegant. The chicken breasts are pounded thin to resemble veal scaloppine, then quickly sautéed. The tart, refreshing pan sauce is simply a reduction of chicken stock, grapefruit juice, and a splash of cream enlivened with pink peppercorns. A garnish of grapefruit sections completes the transformation of the everyday bird into haute cuisine.

⋙

1. Slice each chicken breast on the bias into 3 slices. Using a mallet, flatten each slice of chicken between two sheets of plastic wrap until the breast is about ¼ inch thick. Season the breasts with salt and pepper. Dredge in flour.

2. Heat the vegetable oil in a large nonstick skillet. Cook the chicken until it is golden brown on both sides and cooked through. Transfer it to a platter and keep warm.

3. Add the chicken stock and grapefruit juice to the pan and simmer until the mixture has reduced by half. Add the heavy cream, crème fraîche, and 1 tablespoon of the pink peppercorns, bring to a simmer, and season with salt, white pepper, and tarragon.

4. Pour the sauce over the chicken and garnish with grapefruit sections and the remaining pink peppercorns.

Serves 6

3 boneless, skinless chicken breasts

Salt and freshly ground white pepper to taste

Flour (for dredging)

¼ cup vegetable oil

1 cup chicken stock

¼ cup grapefruit juice

½ cup heavy cream

¼ cup crème fraîche

2 tablespoons pink peppercorns (found in gourmet stores)

2 tablespoons chopped fresh tarragon

2 grapefruits, segmented

Boiled Tenderloin of Beef and Breast of Chicken with Winter Vegetables

Every type of cuisine in the world seems to have its version of a one-pot boiled dinner. The best known are probably the Mongolian firepot and the French pot au feu, *or "pot of fire." The closest American equivalent is the New England boiled dinner.*

Here is a luxurious adaptation featuring tenderloin of beef instead of the lesser cuts of meat typically used. In this recipe the tenderloin can be cooked briefly and served medium rare — unlike the traditional versions where the meat is cooked for hours and emerges somewhat gray.

If you've never tried poaching beef before, you'll be delightfully surprised by the clean, nourishing taste and fabulously buttery texture.

If you plan to serve a group, a whole tenderloin is ideal; however, individual filet mignons may also be used.

Part of the fun and enjoyment of this dish is the zesty garnishes, our favorite being the gremolata — an ancient Italian condiment typically served with osso buco. Gremolata, simply composed of parsley, rosemary, lemon zest, and garlic, is wonderfully versatile and adds sparkle to any food you choose to sprinkle it on.

❧

Serves 6

Poaching Liquid and Broth

¼ cup vegetable oil

1 cup roughly chopped onion

½ cup roughly chopped celery

½ cup roughly chopped carrots

¼ cup tomato paste

1 cup red wine

1 bay leaf

4 sprigs fresh thyme

4 sprigs fresh parsley

1 tablespoon black peppercorns

4 quarts chicken stock

1 tablespoon kosher salt

Gremolata Garnish

¼ cup minced fresh parsley leaves

2 teaspoons grated lemon zest

4 cloves garlic, minced

2 teaspoons minced fresh rosemary, stems removed

For the Poaching Liquid and Broth

1. In a medium-size stockpot, heat the vegetable oil over medium heat. Add the onion, celery, and carrots, and cook until the vegetables begin to soften (about 5 minutes). Add the tomato paste and continue to cook for 5 minutes more.

2. Add the red wine, bay leaf, thyme, parsley, and peppercorns and cook until the wine has almost completely evaporated.

3. Add the chicken stock and salt and simmer for 2 hours, stirring occasionally. Skim any foam that rises to the surface.

4. Strain the broth through a fine mesh sieve. The broth can be prepared several days in advance and stored in the refrigerator until you are ready to cook the boiled beef and chicken.

For the Gremolata Garnish

In a small bowl, combine the parsley, lemon zest, garlic, and rosemary. Set aside. The gremolata garnish can be made several hours ahead of time and kept in the refrigerator until ready to serve.

For the Boiled Beef and Chicken

1. Reserve 3 cups of the poaching liquid to serve with the boiled beef and chicken. Place the remaining poaching liquid in a medium-size stockpot. Add the kosher salt and bring to a simmer.

2. If using a whole beef tenderloin, you may wish to tie the meat with kitchen string to help keep its shape and for easy removal from the cooking liquid. Season the beef with salt and pepper and place in the poaching

liquid. Simmer and cook for 18 to 20 minutes, or until the internal temperature of the meat registers around 125 to 130 degrees on a meat thermometer. Remove the meat from the poaching liquid, cut off the string, and allow to rest in a warm place.

3. Season the chicken breasts with salt and pepper and place in the poaching liquid. Simmer for 4 minutes. Add the carrots, rutabagas, turnips, and potatoes to the poaching liquid and cook for 8 minutes more.

4. Using a slotted spoon, remove the chicken from the poaching liquid.

5. Add the zucchini to the poaching liquid and cook for 2 minutes more, or until the vegetables are tender. Remove all of the vegetables from the liquid with a slotted spoon.

To Serve

1. In a small saucepan, heat 3 cups of the reserved poaching liquid and bring to a boil.

2. Slice each chicken breast and beef filet, and place them in each of 6 serving bowls.

3. Garnish with the cooked vegetables and ladle ½ cup of the reserved poaching liquid into each bowl.

4. Serve the cornichons, Horseradish Cream, Dijon mustard, gremolata, and sea salt on the side in small bowls.

Boiled Beef and Chicken

1 recipe poaching liquid

2 tablespoons kosher salt

1 yard kitchen string (optional)

1 whole beef tenderloin, approximately 5½ pounds (Ask the butcher to trim the meat for you. After trimming, you will end up with a piece of beef weighing about 3½ pounds. Six individual filet mignons weighing about 4 to 6 ounces each may be substituted.)

Salt and freshly ground black pepper to taste

6 boneless, skinless chicken breasts, about 4 ounces each

1 carrot, peeled and cut into ½-inch cubes

1 rutabaga, peeled and cut into ½-inch cubes

1 turnip, peeled and cut into ½-inch cubes

1 potato, peeled and cut into ½-inch cubes

1 zucchini, peeled and cut into ½-inch cubes

To Serve

3 cups of the reserved poaching liquid

18 to 20 whole cornichons

1 recipe Horseradish Cream (see page 214)

⅓ cup whole-grain Dijon mustard

2 tablespoons sea salt

Side Dishes

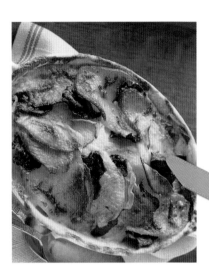

ℰℭ

Little Yellow Grits Soufflés

For some, grits are an acquired taste. Making them into a soufflé definitely widens their appeal. The grits are transformed into something delicate and airy, while retaining their soulful, Southern heritage. This versatile side dish makes a delicious addition to a brunch buffet or an elegant accompaniment for roast chicken, turkey, or pork.

ଜ

Serves 8

For the Molds

8 two-ounce timbale molds
  or miniature muffin tins

1 tablespoon butter, softened

1 tablespoon yellow cornmeal

Soufflés

1 cup milk

⅓ cup yellow corn grits

⅓ cup finely grated Parmesan cheese

½ teaspoon kosher salt

spoon freshly ground black

Pinch of   meg

1 egg yolk

¼ cup heavy cream

3 egg whites

For the Molds

Heavily grease the insides of the timbale molds or miniature muffin tins with softened butter and sprinkle with yellow cornmeal.

For the Soufflés

1. Preheat oven to 375 degrees.

2. In a 1-quart saucepan over medium-high heat, scald the milk. Slowly whisk in the yellow grits. When the grits begin to thicken (after about 3 minutes), stir in the Parmesan cheese. Season with salt, black pepper, and grated nutmeg.

3. Allow the mixture to cool, then stir in the egg yolk and heavy cream.

4. In the bowl of an electric mixer, whip the egg whites on high speed until soft peaks form.

5. Using a rubber spatula, fold the egg whites into the grits mixture.

6. Fill each timbale mold to the top with the batter.

7. Place the molds on a baking sheet and cook in the oven for 10 to 15 minutes, or until set.

8. Remove the soufflés from the oven and allow them to cool for a minute or two. Run a sharp paring knife around the edge of each soufflé and unmold them onto a serving dish or platter.

Bread Pudding Stuffing with Onion Cream Sauce

For years we have tried to lighten and refine Thanksgiving dinner while preserving the rich, soulful flavors we all associate with the day. This savory stuffing is made more delicate by the addition of an egg custard, which gives it the moist, spongelike texture of bread pudding. The puddings are baked in individual molds in a water bath and make a pretty presentation surrounding the turkey. The onion cream sauce, although optional, adds the perfect finishing touch.

Serves 24

Cornbread and Sausage Stuffing

2 pounds bulk pork sausage

6 tablespoons unsalted butter

I large onion, finely chopped

I stalk celery, finely chopped

I Granny Smith apple, peeled, cored, and finely chopped

½ cup chopped pecans

2 cups stale cornbread, crumbled into ¼-inch pieces

4 cups stale white bread, crumbled into ¼-inch pieces

I large egg, lightly beaten

¼ cup applesauce

½ cup turkey or chicken stock

I tablespoon minced fresh sage

I tablespoon minced fresh thyme

2 tablespoons minced fresh celery leaves

Salt and freshly ground black pepper to taste

Onion Cream Sauce

6 tablespoons unsalted butter

4 cups finely chopped onion

4 tablespoons flour

½ cup heavy cream

2 cups milk

Salt and freshly ground white pepper to taste

Freshly grated nutmeg to taste

For the Cornbread and Sausage Stuffing

1. Preheat the oven to 350 degrees.

2. In a large skillet, sauté the sausage over medium heat until it is fully cooked. Drain and set aside.

3. In a large saucepan, melt the butter over medium heat. Add the onion and celery and cook, stirring occasionally, until the onion is translucent. Add the apple, pecans, and sausage. Cook, stirring, for 2 minutes more.

4. Remove from heat and mix in the cornbread and white bread until well combined. Add the egg, applesauce, stock, sage, thyme, celery leaves, salt, and pepper.

5. Transfer the stuffing to a 9 x 12-inch baking pan and cover with foil. Bake for 30 to 40 minutes. Remove from the oven and cool to room temperature. When the stuffing is cool, crumble it into small pieces and set aside. The stuffing can be made in advance and stored in the refrigerator for 2 days.

For the Onion Cream Sauce

1. In a 4-quart saucepan, melt the butter over medium heat. Add the onion and cook, stirring occasionally, until the onion becomes translucent. Add the flour and cook, stirring, for 5 minutes.

2. Meanwhile, in another saucepan, scald the cream and milk together. Whisk the hot cream mixture into the onions and continue whisking until thoroughly combined. Simmer over low heat, stirring occasionally, for 10 minutes. The sauce should be thick enough to coat the back of a spoon. Season with salt, pepper, and nutmeg. Strain the sauce through a fine mesh sieve (if desired). Keep warm until ready to serve.

For the Bread Pudding Stuffing

1. Preheat the oven to 350 degrees.

2. In a mixing bowl, combine the eggs and cream.

3. Grease 24 three-inch ramekins with the butter. Fill each mold ¾ full with the stuffing. Do not pack the stuffing tightly. Pour the egg and cream mixture on top of the stuffing and fill to just below the lip of the ramekins.

4. Set the ramekins in a shallow baking pan and pour enough hot water into the pan to reach 1½ inches up the sides of the ramekins. Bake for 25 to 30 minutes, or until the custard is just set. Remove from the oven and keep warm in the hot water until ready to serve.

5. Unmold the puddings by running the point of a paring knife around the edge of each ramekin. Invert the puddings onto a platter. Nap with the onion cream sauce and pass the remaining sauce in a gravy boat.

Bread Pudding Stuffing

8 large eggs

4 cups heavy cream

Softened butter (for greasing the ramekins)

Potato Gratin with Parsnips and Carrots

Parsnips are one of the most underappreciated vegetables. Their subtle sweetness adds an old-world depth of flavor to this simple gratin. This dish is a delicious accompaniment for a roast leg of lamb and can be partially cooked and assembled ahead of time.

ဆာ

Serves 12

2 tablespoons unsalted butter

½ onion, thinly sliced

2 cups heavy cream

1 cup milk

1 tablespoon kosher salt, or to taste

½ teaspoon freshly ground white pepper

Freshly grated nutmeg to taste

2 large parsnips, peeled and sliced ¼ inch thick

2 large potatoes, peeled and sliced ¼ inch thick

3 large carrots, peeled and sliced on the bias, ¼ inch thick

1. Preheat oven to 375 degrees.

2. In a 4-quart saucepan, melt half of the butter over medium heat. Add the onion and cook, stirring occasionally, for about 5 minutes, or until the onions are wilted and translucent.

3. Add the cream and milk, bring to a boil, and season with salt, pepper, and nutmeg.

4. Fold the parsnips, potatoes, and carrots into the cream mixture with a rubber spatula until each slice is well coated.

5. Simmer the vegetables until the cream mixture begins to thicken and the vegetables are almost tender, about 10 to 15 minutes. They should not be completely cooked.

6. Butter a large shallow baking dish. Pour the vegetable mixture into the dish and dot the top of the vegetables with the remaining butter. The unbaked gratin can be assembled up to this point one day in advance, covered, and refrigerated.

7. Bake in the upper third of the oven for 20 to 25 minutes, or until the top is golden brown and the vegetables are tender.

Wilted Watercress

This tantalizing stir-fry of watercress adds a brilliant color and an Asian accent to poultry or fish dishes.

෨

1. In a large skillet or wok, heat the oil over high heat. Add the watercress; tossing and turning it rapidly with tongs for a few seconds, until the watercress turns brilliant green and just begins to wilt.
2. Sprinkle the Clear Fish Sauce with Lime and Cilantro over the greens, toss with tongs, and remove from heat. Serve immediately.

Serves 6

2 tablespoons vegetable oil

4 bunches watercress, large stems removed, roughly chopped

½ cup Clear Fish Sauce with Lime and Cilantro (see page 212)

Peas and Pearl Onions with Oyster Cream

Thanksgiving dinner would not seem complete without the comforting and familiar side dish of peas and pearl onions. Here is an updated, lighter version of this American holiday classic, made seductive with the flavor of oysters and a hint of curry.

෨

1. Bring a large pot of salted water to a boil. Fill a mixing bowl with ice water and set aside.
2. Place the peas in a strainer or colander small enough to fit into the pot and submerge the peas into the rapidly boiling water. Cook the peas until barely tender — about 5 minutes for fresh peas and 2 minutes for frozen ones. Lift the strainer out of the water and plunge the peas into the ice water to cool thoroughly.
3. To the same pot of boiling water add the pearl onions and cook until tender (about 7 minutes), then drain and add to the peas in the ice water. After the peas and pearl onions are completely chilled, lift them out of the water, drain, and store in the refrigerator until ready to use.
4. In a 4-quart saucepan, melt 1 tablespoon of the butter over medium heat. Add the parsnip, shallot, garlic, country ham, and curry powder and cook for 3 minutes.
5. Add the white wine and oysters and cook until the wine is almost completely evaporated.
6. Add the cream and simmer until the parsnip is soft and the mixture is reduced enough to coat the back of a spoon. Whisk in the remaining butter and strain the oyster cream sauce, pressing hard on the solids to extract maximum flavor.
7. Fold the peas and pearl onions into the cream mixture and warm through before serving. Season with salt and pepper.

Serves 6

3 cups fresh or frozen English peas

1 cup peeled pearl onions

4 tablespoons (½ stick) unsalted butter

1 parsnip, peeled and diced

1 teaspoon diced shallot

1 teaspoon minced garlic

2 slices country ham, diced

⅛ teaspoon curry powder

2 tablespoons dry white wine or vermouth

2 shucked oysters

2 cups heavy cream

Salt and freshly ground black pepper to taste

Shoestring Potatoes

These crispy matchstick potatoes are wonderful with lamb or steak and, unlike French fries, can be cooked well in advance.

෨

Makes about 2 cups

1 large Idaho potato

2 quarts peanut or vegetable oil

Salt to taste

1. Peel the potato and rinse with cold water.
2. Using a mandoline or sharp knife, cut the potato into matchsticks.
3. In a deep fryer or sturdy deep pot, heat the oil to 350 degrees.
4. Dry the potato sticks and carefully sprinkle them into the oil. Cook for 20 to 30 seconds.
5. Using a slotted spoon, remove the potatoes from the oil and drain on paper towels. Sprinkle with salt and store in an airtight container at room temperature in a cool, dry place.

Sweet Corn Relish

This is an enticing addition to a summer picnic or buffet, and makes a perfect accompaniment for crab cakes.

෨

Serves 6

5 ears fresh sweet corn

¼ cup diced red bell pepper

¼ cup diced green bell pepper

1 tablespoon seeded and minced fresh jalapeño pepper

¼ cup diced red onion

2 tablespoons chopped fresh cilantro

2 tablespoons chopped fresh tarragon

¼ cup Tarragon Vinaigrette (see page 220)

Sugar, salt, and freshly ground black pepper to taste

1. Shuck the corn, brushing off all the silk. Strip the kernels from the ears with a sharp knife. You should have about 5 cups of corn.
2. Fill a 4-quart saucepan half full of water, bring to a boil, add the corn, and boil for 2 minutes, or until the kernels are barely tender. Strain the corn through a colander and place in a large mixing bowl.
3. Add the red and green bell peppers, jalapeño, red onion, cilantro, tarragon, and Tarragon Vinaigrette. Mix with a rubber spatula until the ingredients are thoroughly combined.
4. Season with sugar, salt, and pepper. The relish may be made in advance and stored in the refrigerator until ready to serve. The flavor actually improves if the relish is made several hours ahead of time.

Cranberry Salsa

With just the simple addition of a bit of jalapeño pepper and a splash of Grand Marnier, this familiar cranberry relish becomes a sassy salsa. Your turkey will be tapping its drumsticks with delight.

1. Spread the cranberries, orange slices, and jalapeño pepper on a baking sheet and place in the freezer for at least 1 hour.
2. Place the frozen ingredients in a food processor fitted with the blade attachment and pulse repeatedly until everything is evenly minced.
3. Transfer the mixture to a mixing bowl. Fold in the sugar and the Grand Marnier.
4. Cover and refrigerate for at least 24 hours before serving. The salsa can be made up to 5 days ahead of time.

Makes 3 cups

1 pound cranberries, washed and picked through

1 orange, washed, halved, and sliced

1 small fresh jalapeño pepper, ribs and seeds removed

1 cup sugar

2 tablespoons Grand Marnier

Cabbage Braised in Champagne

Here is a simple way to transform a lowly peasant dish of braised cabbage into a refined and elegant fall or winter accompaniment to a roast chicken, goose, or turkey. This side dish is versatile enough to pair with fish and works particularly well with fresh salmon. It can be prepared in less than fifteen minutes and can be kept warm for an hour or so before serving.

1. In a large sauté pan, cook the bacon over medium heat until it is almost crisp. Add the onions and cook, stirring occasionally, for about 5 minutes, until they are translucent.
2. Add the cabbage and cook until it is wilted. Add champagne or white wine, chicken stock, thyme, and cream, and reduce until the liquid thickens enough to coat the back of a spoon.
3. Season with salt and pepper.

Serves 6

3 thick slices bacon, sliced crosswise into ½-inch strips

2 cups thinly sliced onion

4 cups thinly sliced cabbage

½ cup champagne or white wine

¾ cup chicken stock

¼ teaspoon fresh thyme leaves

1 cup heavy cream

Salt and freshly ground black pepper to taste

Desserts

ဆာ

Brioche French Toast with Strawberries and Lemon Verbena Ice Cream

Warm French toast smothered with fresh berries and a scoop of lemon verbena ice cream makes an unforgettably luscious dessert. All of the components can be readied ahead of time. The French toasts can even be fried in advance and rewarmed just before serving. In our kitchen, we make the brioche in miniature bread pans, but any good-quality store-bought brioche will suffice.

Lemon verbena is easy to grow and has become one of our favorite herbs for summer desserts. It's sometimes available at farmer's markets or specialty grocery stores. A good vanilla or buttermilk ice cream may be substituted.

Serves 6

Lemon Verbena Ice Cream

2 cups heavy cream

2 cups whole milk

2 cups fresh lemon verbena leaves

8 egg yolks

1½ cups granulated sugar

Grated zest of 2 lemons

⅔ cup lemon juice

2 tablespoons citron-flavored vodka

Strawberries

2 cups sliced fresh strawberries

Sugar to taste

Brioche French Toast

3 eggs

1½ teaspoons sugar

3 tablespoons milk

2 tablespoons Grand Marnier

1 teaspoon vanilla extract

¼ teaspoon ground cinnamon

12 half-inch-thick brioche slices

2 tablespoons clarified butter

For the Lemon Verbena Ice Cream

1. In a 4-quart, heavy-bottomed saucepan, combine the cream, milk, and lemon verbena over medium heat. Bring to a boil, then remove from heat and allow to steep for approximately 1 hour, or until the cream mixture has a strong lemon verbena flavor. Bring the mixture back to a simmer.

2. Place the egg yolks, sugar, lemon zest, lemon juice, and vodka in the top of a double boiler or in a large stainless steel bowl and slowly whisk in the hot cream mixture. Set the mixture over a pot of simmering water and whisk until the mixture thickens enough to coat the back of a spoon.

3. Remove from heat and strain through a fine mesh sieve.

4. Chill in the refrigerator, then freeze in an ice cream machine according to the manufacturer's instructions.

For the Strawberries

Place the strawberries in a bowl, sweeten them with sugar, and set aside. The strawberries may be prepared several hours in advance and stored in the refrigerator until ready to use.

For the Brioche French Toast

1. In a mixing bowl, whisk the eggs, sugar, milk, Grand Marnier, vanilla extract, and cinnamon together until well combined. The batter may be prepared in advance and stored overnight in the refrigerator.

2. Drop the brioche slices into the egg mixture and allow them to soak for one minute.

3. Meanwhile, on a griddle or in a nonstick pan, heat the clarified butter over medium-high heat. Carefully lift the brioche slices from the batter and let the excess batter drain off. Fry the brioche slices until golden brown on each side, about 30 seconds per side.

4. Place 2 pieces of brioche French toast on each of 6 serving plates. Pile ⅓ cup of sliced, sugared strawberries on top of each portion of French toast. Place a scoop of lemon verbena ice cream on top of the strawberries.

Strawberry-Rhubarb Shortcake with Crème Fraîche Ice Cream

Rhubarb is an underappreciated springtime treasure. These shortcakes can be served in miniature along with Rhubarb Sorbet (see page 180) and a Gingered Rhubarb Tart (see page 181), illustrating the versatility of this old-timey garden "pie fruit." While the tastes of grandmother's kitchen are evoked in each mouthful, this presentation keeps the palate intrigued and the waistline intact.

For the Crème Fraîche Ice Cream

1. In a medium-size saucepan, combine the milk, sugar, and lemon zest, bring to a boil, and remove from heat.

2. Place the egg yolks in the top of a double boiler or in a large stainless steel bowl and slowly whisk in the hot milk mixture. Set the mixture over a pot of simmering water and whisk until it thickens enough to coat the back of a spoon.

3. Remove from heat and strain through a fine mesh sieve. Stir in the lemon juice and crème fraîche.

4. Chill in the refrigerator, then freeze in an ice cream machine according to the manufacturer's instructions.

For the Strawberry-Rhubarb Compote

1. In a 2-quart saucepan, combine the rhubarb, sugar, and water. Bring to a boil over medium heat.

2. Reduce heat and simmer for 15 minutes, or until the rhubarb is soft.

3. Remove from heat, puree in a blender, and cool completely.

4. Add the strawberries and store in the refrigerator until ready to serve.

For the Shortcake

1. Preheat the oven to 350 degrees.

2. Line a cookie sheet with parchment paper.

3. In a food processor, grind the toasted almonds to a fine powder.

4. In the bowl of an electric mixer fitted with a paddle attachment, combine the ground almonds, flour, sugar, baking powder, and butter on low speed. With the mixer running, add 1 cup of heavy cream in a steady stream. Mix until just barely combined. If the dough appears to be a bit dry, add a little more cream. Stop mixing as soon as the dough comes together and forms a ball.

5. Roll out the dough on a floured surface to ½ inch thick. Cut the shortcake dough into 2-inch squares and place them on the parchment-lined cookie sheet. Bake for 10 to 15 minutes, until the shortcakes are just barely golden on the edges. Cool on a wire rack.

Continued on page 180

Makes 24 miniature shortcakes

Crème Fraîche Ice Cream

Zest and juice of 1 lemon

2 cups milk

1 cup sugar

7 egg yolks

2 cups crème fraîche

Strawberry-Rhubarb Compote

6 stalks of fresh rhubarb, roughly chopped

¾ cup sugar

½ cup water

1 pint strawberries, diced

Shortcake

¾ cup slivered almonds, toasted

3 cups cake flour

½ cup confectioners' sugar

2 tablespoons baking powder

¼ pound (1 stick) cold butter, cut into cubes

1 cup plus 2 tablespoons heavy cream, cold

To Assemble and Serve

1. Split the shortcakes in half crosswise.

2. Place the bottom half of each shortcake in the center of each serving plate.

3. Place a scoop of crème fraîche ice cream on top of the shortcake, ladle the strawberry-rhubarb compote over the ice cream, and place the top half of the shortcake on top of the ice cream and compote.

Rhubarb Sorbet

The addition of a cup of raspberries to this sorbet intensifies the rhubarb's vibrant red color and helps balance its natural sourness.

ॐ

Makes 1½ quarts

12 thick stalks rhubarb

2 cups water

1½ cups sugar

1 cup raspberries

1. Wash the rhubarb, trim off any leaves, and cut out any brown or bruised spots. Using a sharp knife, roughly chop the rhubarb.

2. In a 4-quart saucepan, combine the chopped rhubarb, water, sugar, and raspberries. Bring to a boil and cook until the rhubarb is very soft.

3. In a blender, puree the rhubarb mixture in batches. Strain through a fine mesh sieve to remove fiber and seeds. Taste and add more sugar if needed. Chill.

4. Freeze in an ice cream machine according to the manufacturer's instructions.

Gingered Rhubarb Tarts

Rhubarb always seems to bring back memories of old-fashioned deep-dish pies oozing their hot juices in springtimes long past. These delicate miniature tarts are slathered with a gingered rhubarb puree and covered with thin slices of sweetened rhubarb before baking. They emerge warm and fragrant from the oven, screaming for a scoop of ice cream.

❧

1. On a floured board, roll the dough out to about ⅛ inch thick. Lay a bowl about 5 inches in diameter upside down on the dough and, using the rim as a pattern, cut out six circles with a sharp paring knife. Place the pastry rounds between sheets of waxed paper and refrigerate.

2. In a 4-quart saucepan, combine the water, sugar, and sliced ginger root, bring to a boil, and simmer until the sugar is dissolved. Remove from heat.

3. Wash the rhubarb, trim off any leaves, and cut out brown or bruised spots.

4. Using a very sharp knife, slice six of the stalks on the bias, about ⅛ inch thick. Place the slices in a stainless steel bowl, carefully pour 2 cups of the sugar syrup over them, and set aside.

5. Roughly chop the remaining four stalks of rhubarb and add them to the remaining syrup. Simmer the mixture over medium heat until the rhubarb is soft, remove from heat, and strain, reserving the liquid. Remove the ginger root and puree the rhubarb in a food processor or blender. Add enough raspberry puree to the rhubarb to give it a reddish tint. Chill the puree until you are ready to assemble the tarts.

6. Reduce the reserved liquid to a syrupy consistency to glaze tarts after baking.

To Assemble the Tarts

1. Preheat the oven to 375 degrees.

2. Remove the pastry rounds from the refrigerator. Spray several baking sheets with nonstick cooking spray and lay the pastry rounds on top of them. Spread about 1 tablespoon of the rhubarb puree evenly over each round. Lift the rhubarb slices out of their liquid and arrange them on top of the puree in a single layer of concentric circles.

3. Bake the tarts in the lower half of the oven for 10 to 15 minutes, or until the pastry is crisp and golden brown. Remove from the oven and, using a pastry brush, glaze each tart with the reduced syrup. Serve warm.

Serves 6

1 recipe Basic Pie Dough (see page 200; croissant dough or puff pastry may be substituted)

1 quart water

1½ cups sugar

2 thin slices fresh ginger root, unpeeled

10 thick stalks red rhubarb

2 to 3 tablespoons Raspberry Puree (see page 186)

Warm Plum Torte with Sweet Corn Ice Cream

This old-world cakelike torte will put your palate in a time machine and take you back to your great-grandmother's little farm in the country. The sweet-tart plums are enveloped in a buttermilk batter with brown sugar streusel topping, and served warm and fragrant.

Serves 8

Crumb Topping

⅓ cup all-purpose flour

4 teaspoons chopped walnuts

2 tablespoons granulated sugar

1 tablespoon brown sugar

Pinch of ground cinnamon

Pinch of ground cardamom

2 tablespoons melted butter

Plum Torte

1 cup pitted, diced fresh red plums

½ cup sugar

⅛ cup plum liqueur

Nonstick cooking spray

¼ pound (1 stick) unsalted butter, at room temperature

2 tablespoons brown sugar

½ cup sugar

2 eggs

½ cup buttermilk

½ teaspoon vanilla extract

1 teaspoon orange zest

1 cup all-purpose flour

¾ teaspoon baking soda

Sweet Corn Ice Cream (see below)

For the Crumb Topping

1. Combine the flour, walnuts, sugar, brown sugar, cinnamon, and cardamom in a food processor and pulse to combine.

2. Add the butter and process until the mixture resembles coarse meal. The crumb topping may be made several days in advance and stored in the refrigerator.

For the Plum Torte

1. In a mixing bowl, combine the plums, sugar, and plum liqueur. Set aside. The plum mixture may be prepared ahead of time and stored in the refrigerator overnight.

2. Preheat the oven to 350 degrees. Spray a 9-inch pie pan with nonstick cooking spray and set aside.

3. In the bowl of an electric mixer, beat the butter, brown sugar, and sugar together on high speed until light and fluffy.

4. With the mixer on low speed, add the eggs one at a time and beat to combine. Add the buttermilk, vanilla, and orange zest. When thoroughly combined, slowly add the flour and baking soda, scraping down the sides, and mix until the batter is smooth.

5. Pour the batter into the prepared pie pan. Drain the plums and arrange them on top of the batter. Sprinkle the crumb topping over the plums.

6. Place the pie pan on a cookie sheet and bake it in the oven for 45 minutes, or until the torte is golden brown. Transfer the torte to a wire rack and let cool.

7. When ready to serve, rewarm the torte and serve it with Sweet Corn Ice Cream.

Sweet Corn Ice Cream

Every year, in celebration of the summer's sweet corn harvest, we look forward to composing a menu using corn in novel ways with every course. This intriguing ice cream emphasizes the corn's natural sweetness and creamy texture. It's an especially good accompaniment with summer fruit pies and cobblers.

1. In a 4-quart heavy-bottomed saucepan, combine the milk, cream, sugar, corn kernels, and corncobs over medium heat. Bring to a boil, then remove from heat and allow the cream mixture to steep for approximately 1 hour, or until it tastes like sweet corn.

2. Strain the cream mixture through a fine mesh strainer and bring the mixture back to a simmer. Discard the corn kernels and cobs.

3. Place the eggs and egg yolks in the top of a double boiler or in a large stainless steel bowl and slowly whisk in the hot cream mixture. Set the mixture over a pot of simmering water and whisk until it thickens enough to coat the back of a spoon. Remove from heat and stir in the maple syrup.

4. Chill in the refrigerator, then freeze in an ice cream machine according to the manufacturer's instructions.

Makes about 1¾ quarts

2 cups milk

4 cups heavy cream

1½ cups granulated sugar

4 ears sweet corn, shucked, kernels removed, cobs reserved and broken in half

7 eggs

2 egg yolks

4 tablespoons maple syrup

Our Virginia Peach Melba

Legendary chef Auguste Escoffier reputedly first named a raspberry-sauced, poached peach and ice cream dessert after the Australian opera singer Nellie Melba in 1892. For good reason, the combination of raspberry sauce, peaches, and ice cream has remained popular to this day. Our version has the peach resting on a disk of almond-scented cake and a layer of buttermilk ice cream, with a crisscross of raspberry puree.

⁊ꙩ

For the Cake

1. Preheat the oven to 375 degrees.

2. Spray a 15½ x 10½-inch baking sheet with nonstick cooking spray. Line the sheet with parchment paper and spray again. Dust lightly with flour.

3. In the bowl of an electric mixer fitted with a paddle attachment, beat the butter and sugar together until light and fluffy. Add the egg yolks, one at a time, followed by the almond extract and milk.

4. With the mixer on low speed, slowly add the flour, baking powder, and salt and mix until the batter is smooth.

5. Pour the batter into the prepared baking sheet and spread evenly into all four corners. Bake the cake for 10 to 12 minutes, or until the cake is set.

6. Run a knife around the edges of the cake to loosen it from the sheet. Cool the cake on a wire rack.

For the Buttermilk Ice Cream

1. Line a baking sheet (exactly the same size as the one you used to bake the cake) with plastic wrap.

2. In a 4-quart, heavy-bottomed saucepan, combine the milk, cream, sugar, and vanilla bean over medium heat. Bring to a boil and remove from heat.

3. Place the egg yolks in the top of a double boiler or in a large stainless steel bowl and slowly whisk in the hot cream mixture. Set the mixture over a pot of simmering water and whisk until the mixture thickens enough to coat the back of a spoon.

4. Remove from heat and strain through a fine mesh sieve.

5. Add the buttermilk and chill in the refrigerator. Freeze in an ice cream machine according to the manufacturer's instructions.

6. Working quickly, spread the buttermilk ice cream out over the plastic wrap in the baking sheet, about ½ inch deep. Immediately place the sheet of ice cream in the freezer and freeze until stiff, about 3 hours.

For the Peaches

1. In a heavy-bottomed saucepan, combine the water and sugar over medium heat. Stir until the sugar has completely dissolved and the liquid is clear.

2. Meanwhile, halve, pit, and peel the peaches. Place the peach halves in a large heat-proof bowl.

Serves 8

Cake

Nonstick cooking spray

Flour for dusting

6 ounces (1½ sticks) soft butter, unsalted

¾ cup sugar

3 egg yolks

½ teaspoon almond extract

½ cup milk, at room temperature

1½ cups cake flour

1 teaspoon baking powder

¼ teaspoon salt

Buttermilk Ice Cream

2 cups milk

2 cups heavy cream

1⅓ cups sugar

½ vanilla bean, split lengthwise

5 egg yolks

1¼ cups buttermilk

Peaches

4½ cups water

2 cups sugar

4 ripe peaches

Continued on page 186

3. Pour the hot liquid over the peach halves. The peaches may be prepared in advance, stored in the liquid, and refrigerated for several days.

To Assemble and Serve the Peach Melbas

Garnishes

½ cup Raspberry Puree (see below)

½ cup sliced, toasted almonds

1. Remove the ice cream from the freezer. Using the edges of the plastic wrap, lift the ice cream out of the pan, invert it on top of the cake, and remove the plastic wrap.

2. Using a fluted 2½-inch round cutter, cut out 8 rounds of ice cream and cake. Any remaining cake and ice cream may be stored in the freezer for another use. Place a peach half on top of each ice cream–cake round. Using a spatula, transfer the peach melba to the center of each of 8 serving plates. Drizzle the Raspberry Puree over each peach half and garnish with toasted almonds.

Raspberry Puree

Makes 1 cup

3 pints fresh raspberries

1 tablespoon fresh lemon juice

3 to 4 tablespoons sugar

1. Puree the berries in a food processor. Strain through a fine mesh sieve to remove all the seeds, pressing hard on the solids with a rubber spatula to remove all the liquid.

2. Add the lemon juice and mix well.

3. Add the sugar, 1 tablespoon at a time, tasting after each addition, until the desired sweetness is obtained.

Human Dog Biscuits

While our guests are at dinner, their beds are turned down and they receive a note wishing them sweet dreams from our Dalmatian mascots. With the note are these miniature, crunchy, bone-shaped shortbread cookies. These "human dog biscuits" are meant to be dipped, like biscotti, in a glass of port.

ℬↄ

1. In a small saucepan over medium heat, melt the butter, stirring constantly. Increase the heat and continue stirring as the butter foams and begins to turn golden brown. Immediately remove the butter from heat and carefully pour it into a heat-proof container.

2. In the bowl of an electric mixer, beat the sugar and eggs until light and airy.

3. With the mixer on low speed, slowly add the browned butter and Amaretto. Slowly add the flour, ground almonds, and ginger, and mix until the dough is smooth. Form the dough into a ball, wrap it in plastic wrap, and chill it for 30 minutes.

4. Preheat the oven to 350 degrees. Line two baking sheets with parchment paper or spray with nonstick cooking spray.

5. On a lightly floured board, roll out the dough to about ⅓ inch thick. Using a bone-shaped cookie cutter, cut out the cookies and place them on the baking sheets.

6. Bake for about 10 to 15 minutes, or until the cookies are just golden brown. Serve with a glass of port to dip the cookies in.

Makes 36 three-inch cookies

¼ pound (1 stick) lightly salted butter, cut into tablespoon-size pieces

1 cup sugar

2 eggs

2 tablespoons Amaretto

2¾ cups all-purpose flour

1½ cups whole almonds, finely ground

2 tablespoons minced candied ginger (available in the gourmet section of your supermarket)

Nonstick cooking spray

Chocolate-Mint Fantasy

This dazzling finale features a wonderfully refreshing mint ice cream that you will definitely want to add to your ice cream–making repertoire. The chocolate curls take a bit of practice but can be made well in advance and kept in the freezer.

ৎ∽

For the Mint Ice Cream

1. In a 2-quart heavy-bottomed saucepan, combine the milk, cream, sugar, and mint over medium heat. Bring to a boil, then remove from heat and allow to steep for approximately one hour, or until the cream mixture has a peppermint flavor. Remove the peppermint. Bring the cream mixture back to a simmer.

2. Place the egg yolks in the top of a double boiler or in a large stainless steel bowl and slowly whisk in the hot cream mixture. Set the mixture over a pot of simmering water and whisk until the mixture thickens enough to coat the back of a spoon.

3. Remove from heat and strain through a fine mesh sieve. Stir in the crème de menthe.

4. Chill in the refrigerator, then freeze in an ice cream machine according to the manufacturer's instructions.

For the Chocolate Ribbons

1. Roughly chop the chocolate with a chef's knife and place it in a stainless steel bowl. Place the bowl over a pot of barely simmering water, making sure that no moisture comes in contact with the chocolate. Stir the chocolate occasionally until it is about half melted. Remove from heat and whisk until all of the chocolate has melted and is very smooth.

2. Using an offset metal cake spatula, spread about ¼ cup of the melted chocolate out on the back of a cookie sheet. The chocolate should be only ⅛ to ¹⁄₁₆ inch thick.

3. Place the cookie sheet in the freezer for about 30 seconds to allow the chocolate to set up slightly and just begin to dry. Using a knife, cut the chocolate into 2-inch-wide ribbons.

4. Using a wide putty knife or metal pastry scraper held at a 45-degree angle, scrape the ribbons off of the cookie sheet, forming irregularly shaped curls.

5. Place the chocolate curls in the freezer to solidify for a few more seconds. Cover and store the curls in a container in the freezer until ready to serve.

To Serve

1. Several hours before serving, smooth the mint ice cream into the wells of frozen soup plates or serving bowls and return them to the freezer.

2. Just before serving, remove the ice cream and the chocolate curls from the freezer and mound the curls on top of the ice cream.

Makes about 1¾ quarts

Mint Ice Cream

2 cups whole milk

2 cups heavy cream

1 cup sugar

¼ pound fresh peppermint (about 2 bunches)

8 egg yolks

2 tablespoons crème de menthe

Chocolate Ribbons

¼ pound finest-quality semisweet chocolate

A Pear Trio: Pear Sorbet, Pear Tart, and Fallen Pear Soufflé

We like the idea of showcasing the many dimensions of a fruit by featuring it in a trio of small desserts. In this case, we offer a miniature pear tart in the shape of a pear, a fallen pear soufflé, and a pear-shaped pear sorbet. While each dish complements the others, all of them are capable of standing alone. If you wish to serve them together, you should definitely make the pear sorbet a day in advance. Happily, the fallen pear soufflé can be baked hours in advance and rewarmed just before serving.

ℰℴ

Serves 8

Pear Sorbet

4 ripe pears

1½ cups Simple Syrup (see page 218)

1 tablespoon fresh lemon juice

8 sprigs mint

For the Pear Sorbet

1. Peel, core, and roughly chop the pears. Using a blender or food processor, puree the pears until they are completely smooth. You should have about 2 cups of pear puree.

2. In a medium-size bowl, combine the pureed pears, Simple Syrup, and lemon juice.

3. Transfer the mixture to an ice cream machine and freeze according to the manufacturer's instructions. Remove the sorbet from the ice cream machine and place in the freezer for 2 hours or overnight.

4. If you desire, the pear sorbet can be made into little pear shapes. Simply scoop 8 balls of sorbet with a small ice cream scoop and then, using a melon-ball scoop, place a smaller ball of sorbet on top of each one. Return them to the freezer for half an hour. Then, using the back of a spoon, smooth the surface of the 2 balls into rounded pear shapes. Freeze the miniature pears until ready to serve. Just before serving, a sprig of mint can be placed as a stem on the top of each little pear.

Pear Tart

1 recipe Basic Pie Dough
(see page 200; croissant dough or puff pastry may be substituted)

4 pears, peeled, halved, and cored

4½ cups water

2 cups sugar

3 whole star anise

1 three-inch cinnamon stick

Nonstick cooking spray

½ cup pear or apple jelly

For the Pear Tart

1. On a floured board, roll the dough out to about ⅛ inch thick. Using a 3-inch pear-shaped cookie cutter or a 4½-inch round cutter, cut out eight pieces of dough. Place the pastry between sheets of plastic wrap and refrigerate.

2. In a heavy-bottomed saucepan, combine the pear halves, water, sugar, star anise, and cinnamon over medium heat. Simmer until the pears are tender when pierced with a paring knife. Remove from heat.

3. Using a slotted spoon, lift the pears from the liquid and cool them on a plate or wire rack.

4. Preheat the oven to 375 degrees.

5. Spray several cookie sheets with nonstick cooking spray. Remove the pastry cut-outs from the refrigerator and lay them on top of the cookie sheets. Prick each one several times with a fork.

6. Slice each halved pear lengthwise into ¼-inch slices. Fan the slices out on top of each piece of pastry.

Continued on page 192

7. Bake the tarts in the lower half of the oven for 10 to 15 minutes, or until the pastry is crisp and golden brown. Remove from the oven. Meanwhile, in a small saucepan, melt the pear or apple jelly over low heat.

8. Using a pastry brush, brush each tart with the melted jelly.

For the Soufflé Molds

3 tablespoons soft butter

8 two-ounce timbale molds or miniature muffin tins

4 tablespoons sugar

Fallen Pear Soufflé

2 ripe pears

3 tablespoons pear brandy or eau de vie, such as Poire Williams

¼ cup sugar

3 egg whites

For the Soufflé Molds

Butter the insides of the molds or muffin tins and sprinkle them with sugar.

For the Fallen Pear Soufflé

1. Preheat the oven to 375 degrees.

2. Peel, core, and roughly chop the pears. Using a blender or food processor, puree the pears until they are completely smooth. You should have about 1 cup of pear puree.

3. In a mixing bowl, combine the pear puree, pear brandy, and half of the sugar.

4. In the bowl of an electric mixer fitted with the whisk attachment, whip the egg whites on high speed until they begin to form soft peaks. With the mixer running, add the remaining half of the sugar in a steady stream and continue whipping until the egg whites form stiff peaks.

5. Using a rubber spatula, fold the egg whites into the pear puree mixture.

6. Pour the soufflé batter into the prepared molds. Place the molds in a baking pan with 2-inch sides. Place the baking pan in the oven and carefully pour hot water around the soufflés until it reaches halfway up the sides of the molds. Bake for 10 to 12 minutes, until the soufflés are golden brown and set.

Garnishes

I recipe Caramel Sauce (see below)

8 Pear Chips (see page 193)

To Assemble and Serve

1. Run a sharp paring knife around the edge of the soufflés and unmold one onto each serving plate.

2. Place a pear tart next to it and pool a little Caramel Sauce on the side. If desired (to help keep the pear sorbet from sliding) place a Pear Chip next to the pear tart and slip a pear-shaped sorbet onto the center of each chip.

Caramel Sauce

Makes 2¼ cups

I½ cups sugar

½ cup water

I cup heavy cream

¼ pound (I stick) butter

1. In a large saucepan, caramelize the sugar and water. Remove from heat.

2. Heat the cream and slowly whisk into the caramel. Be careful of rising steam.

3. Whisk in small pieces of softened butter. Cool.

ᔆᑏ

Pear Chips

These attractive, crisp pear chips make a dressy garnish for a fall dessert.

1. Preheat the oven to 250 degrees.
2. Using a sharp knife or mandoline, slice the whole pear lengthwise into ⅛-inch slices, including the core. (Don't worry about the seeds; they can be removed after the pears are baked. The core will become edible.)
3. Bring the Simple Syrup to a boil and add the pear slices. Remove from heat and let the pears soak in the syrup for 30 minutes.
4. Using a slotted spoon, lift the pear slices out of the syrup, drain well, lay them on a nonstick baking sheet or one lined with a Silpat sheet, and blot the excess liquid with a paper towel. Cover with another Silpat of the same size and weight it with the bottom of a matching baking sheet.
5. Bake for 1 hour. Remove from the oven, lift the top baking sheet and Silpat, turn the pear slices over, cover with the Silpat and baking sheet, and return to the oven for 1 more hour, or until the chips are dried and crisp. Remove the pear slices from the pan and lay them on a wire rack to cool and dry. They may be stored in an airtight container at room temperature for several days.

Makes about 15 chips

1 fresh firm pear
2 cups Simple Syrup (see page 218)

Caramelized Banana Tart

Your guests will go ape over this warm banana tart. A disk of flaky pastry is spread with banana-flavored custard, layered with sliced bananas, then sprinkled with sugar and caramelized. We use a blowtorch to melt the sugar and create a crackling, caramel glaze over the banana slices, but a hot broiler will achieve almost the same effect. Toasted macadamia nuts are sprinkled on the tarts for additional flavor and crunch. The tropical theme can be further accentuated with a scoop of coconut ice cream melting on top. All of the components can be readied in advance for last-minute assembly.

❧

Serves 6

Roasted Banana Pastry Cream

1 tablespoon vegetable oil

2 ripe bananas, unpeeled

2¼ cups milk

⅔ cup sugar

2 eggs

4 egg yolks

¼ cup all-purpose flour

4 tablespoons (½ stick) unsalted butter

2 tablespoons banana liqueur (optional)

Pastry

1 recipe Basic Pie Dough (see page 200; croissant dough or puff pastry may be substituted)

Nonstick cooking spray

To Serve

6 ripe bananas

6 tablespoons sugar

¼ cup macadamia nuts, toasted and roughly chopped

Coconut Ice Cream (see page 196)

For the Roasted Banana Pastry Cream

1. Preheat the oven to 350 degrees.

2. Lightly oil the bananas in their skins and place them on a baking sheet. Bake for 10 to 15 minutes, or until the skins are blackened. Remove the bananas from the oven and peel. Puree in a food processor.

3. In a medium-size saucepan, bring the banana puree, milk, and ⅓ cup of the sugar to a boil over medium heat and set aside.

4. In a stainless steel saucepan, whisk the eggs, egg yolks, flour, and the remaining sugar together. Slowly whisk in the hot milk and banana mixture. Cook over medium heat, whisking constantly until the mixture thickens and just comes to a boil. Remove from heat.

5. Whisk in the butter and banana liqueur.

6. Refrigerate until ready to use.

For the Pastry

1. On a floured board, roll the dough out to about ⅛ inch thick. Lay a bowl about 5 inches in diameter upside down on the dough and, using the rim as a pattern, cut out six circles with a sharp paring knife. Place the pastry rounds between sheets of waxed paper and refrigerate.

2. Preheat the oven to 375 degrees.

3. Remove the pastry rounds from the refrigerator. Spray two baking sheets with nonstick cooking spray and lay the pastry rounds on top of them. Using the tines of a fork, prick the pastry rounds at half-inch intervals.

4. Bake the pastry in the lower half of the oven for 10 to 12 minutes, or until it is crisp and golden brown. Cool.

To Serve

1. Spread about 1½ tablespoons of roasted banana pastry cream evenly over each round.

2. Peel and slice the bananas on an angle. Arrange them in a single layer of concentric circles on top of the pastry cream.

3. Sprinkle each tart evenly with 1 tablespoon of sugar.

Continued on page 196

4. Hold a lit blowtorch about 6 inches from the top of each tart and move the flame evenly over the surface of the bananas, allowing the sugar to melt and caramelize. Let cool for several minutes to let the sugar harden. Sprinkle each tart with macadamia nuts.

5. Serve warm with a scoop of Coconut Ice Cream.

Coconut Ice Cream

This is a relatively easy-to-make, wonderfully rich, tropical ice cream. It can be whimsically presented by packing it into little coconut "shells" made of chocolate. The shells are made by dipping a blown-up balloon halfway into melted chocolate, rolling it in nuts, letting the chocolate set, and popping the balloon. The chocolate shell can then be filled with ice cream.

Makes 2 quarts

Coconut Ice Cream

4 cups whole milk

2 cups heavy cream

1 cup granulated sugar

7 egg yolks

1½ cans (3¾ cups) cream of coconut, such as Coco López

Coconut "Shells" (optional)

8 small balloons

2 cups chopped semisweet chocolate, melted

1 cup chopped macadamia nuts

For the Coconut Ice Cream

1. In a 4-quart heavy-bottomed saucepan, combine the milk, cream, and sugar over medium heat. Bring to a boil and remove from heat.

2. Place the egg yolks and cream of coconut in the top of a double boiler or in a large stainless steel bowl and slowly whisk in the hot cream mixture. Set the mixture over a pot of simmering water and whisk until the mixture thickens enough to coat the back of a spoon.

3. Remove from heat and strain through a fine mesh sieve.

4. Chill in the refrigerator, then freeze in an ice cream machine according to the manufacturer's instructions.

To make the Coconut "Shells" (optional)

1. Line a cookie sheet with waxed paper or parchment paper.

2. Blow up the balloons and dip each one halfway in the melted chocolate, then roll the bottoms in the nuts. Rest the dipped balloons on the prepared cookie sheet and place in the freezer until the chocolate hardens, about 30 minutes.

3. Take the balloons out of the freezer and pop them with the tip of a knife. Remove the balloon and carefully fill each shell with the coconut ice cream, smoothing the top of each scoop with a knife. Return the filled shells to the freezer until hardened.

4. Using a melon-ball scoop, scoop out an indentation in the center of the ice cream in each coconut half. (Save the small scoops of ice cream and combine them with the remaining ice cream and keep frozen.) The coconut halves can be made several days in advance and kept covered in the freezer until ready to serve.

Rosemary Shortbread

The unexpected addition of fresh rosemary turns this classic shortbread tea cookie into something unique and memorable. You may wish to experiment with other fresh herbs, such as lemon verbena, mint, or tarragon. (Dried herbs are not recommended.)

৪১

1. In the bowl of an electric mixer fitted with a paddle attachment, combine the butter, confectioners' sugar, rosemary, and salt on low speed.
2. Gradually add the flour and mix just until it's incorporated.
3. Wrap the dough in plastic wrap and chill for 30 minutes.
4. Preheat the oven to 300 degrees. Line a baking sheet with parchment paper.
5. On a lightly floured surface, roll the dough out until it is about ⅓ inch thick. Using a 1½-inch round cookie cutter, cut out circles of dough.
6. Place the rounds of shortbread on the lined baking sheet and bake for 15 minutes. (They should remain pale in color.)

Makes 60 cookies

10 ounces (2½ sticks) butter

¼ cup confectioners' sugar

1½ teaspoons chopped fresh rosemary, stemmed

¼ teaspoon salt

2½ cups all-purpose flour

Banana Yogurt Sorbet

Not quite an ice cream, not quite a sorbet, this frozen yogurt treat requires no cooking and happily combines with fresh fruit for a light and refreshing summer dessert.

৪১

1. Puree all of the ingredients in a blender.
2. Freeze in an ice cream machine according to the manufacturer's instructions.

Makes 1½ quarts

4 ripe medium-size bananas

3¼ cups plain yogurt

1 cup heavy cream

1 cup sugar

Pineapple Skillet Tarts

As a child, I always loved my mother's pineapple upside-down cake. But as a chef, I knew it needed a drastic makeover to take it into the next century. Losing the Maraschino cherry was a no-brainer. Getting rid of the cake's clunkiness was trickier.

I remembered a caramelized Alsatian apple crepe we used to serve, and instead of using apples, tried substituting thinly sliced pineapple. The pineapple's acidity made the dessert more refreshing, and surprisingly, all of the flavors I remembered from childhood were preserved in something light and delicate.

The crepe is a six-inch disk with thin slices of pineapple laid in concentric circles and covered with an alluring golden glaze. The caramelization created in the skillet tastes just like the gooey brown-sugar topping on the American classic.

People are sometimes afraid to make crepes because they think the crepes have to be paper thin. However, this dish will be equally delicious if the crepes are more like pancakes.

Flipping them will take a little practice. The trick is to jerk the pan forward with a quick flipping motion, then catch the crepe as it lands upside down. (People usually don't thrust the pan forward with enough oomph.) If you're worried about watching the first few crepes fall on the floor, ask the dog to stand by when you practice, or put a plate over the pan, invert the pancake onto the plate, then return it to the pan, pineapple side down.

It would seem like torture if you made the tarts while your guests were waiting or watching, but there is really no point in doing this. You can make them in advance and warm them on greased cookie sheets before serving.

ဆ

Serves 10 to 12

Crepe Batter

2 cups all-purpose flour

6 tablespoons unsalted butter, melted and cooled

¼ cup sugar

3 eggs

Pinch of salt

1 cup milk, or as needed

Skillet Tarts

2 large ripe pineapples, peeled, cored, and cut lengthwise into quarters

6 tablespoons (¾ stick) unsalted butter

¾ cup toasted, coarsely ground macadamia nuts

½ cup sugar

¾ cup heavy cream

Nonstick cooking spray

For the Crepe Batter

1. Combine the flour, melted butter, sugar, eggs, and salt in a food processor or blender.

2. With the motor running, add enough milk (about 1 cup) to make a fluid batter. The batter may be covered and refrigerated for up to 24 hours.

For the Skillet Tarts

1. Line two baking sheets with parchment paper and set aside.

2. Slice the pineapple quarters crosswise, ⅛ inch thick.

3. In a 7-inch nonstick pan over medium heat, melt ¼ teaspoon of the butter, spreading with a spatula. Remove the pan.

4. With the pan off the heat, ladle about 3 tablespoons of batter into the pan and roll it around until the bottom of the pan is evenly coated with the batter. Sprinkle the crepe with 1 tablespoon of the macadamia nuts.

5. Return the pan to medium heat. Just as the crepe begins to set but is still wet on top, remove the pan from heat and arrange pineapple slices in an

Continued on page 200

overlapping circular pattern, completely covering the surface of the crepe. Use a skewer or fork to arrange any of the pineapple slices that fall out of place. Shake the crepe slightly to keep it from sticking to the pan.

6. Return the pan to heat and sprinkle the pineapple with 2 teaspoons of sugar and about ½ tablespoon of cold butter, cut into bits. Use a rubber spatula to loosen the edge of the crepe and check the underside. When the bottom is golden brown, loosen the crepe by running a rubber spatula around the edges, and carefully flip the crepe over in the pan. Continue cooking until the sugar underneath turns a light caramel color. Add 1 tablespoon of cream around the edges of the crepe and tilt the pan so the cream blends with the sugar and runs under the crepe.

7. Spray a flat metal surface, such as the bottom of a cake pan, with nonstick cooking spray. Place the sprayed side over the tart and invert the pan to remove the tart. Slide the tart onto a prepared baking sheet. Repeat the process, wiping the pan clean between tarts, to make 10 to 12. The sheet of tarts may be covered and refrigerated for up to 4 hours.

Garnishes

½ cup 151-proof rum (optional, for flaming the tarts)

1 recipe Coconut Ice Cream (see page 196)

To Serve

1. Reheat the tarts in a 350-degree oven until hot, about 4 minutes. Transfer to serving plates.

2. Pour the rum into a small heat-proof pitcher or gravy boat and set aflame.

3. Carefully spoon the burning rum over the tarts in a darkened dining room.

4. Serve with Coconut Ice Cream.

Basic Pie Dough

Makes one 9- to 10-inch crust

2 cups all-purpose flour

⅓ cup butter

⅓ cup shortening or vegetable oil

⅓ cup ice water

1. Sift the flour into a medium-size bowl. Add the butter and shortening or oil, and cut into small pieces with a pastry cutter or two knives. Work the mixture with your fingertips until it resembles coarse cornmeal.

2. Make a well in the center of the mixture and add the water, kneading until the dough forms a ball.

3. Wrap the dough tightly in plastic wrap and refrigerate for at least 30 minutes.

4. When you're ready to use the dough, roll it out on a lightly floured surface and proceed with your recipe.

Frozen Eggnog Soufflé

If you're like me, you're always looking for a novel way to present a traditional holiday dessert that can be made in advance. Something cold and refreshing offers a welcome ending to a sumptuous feast, and nothing captures the Yuletide spirit as well as the taste of homemade eggnog. This frozen fantasy soufflé looks as if you just pulled it out of the oven, but in reality you just slipped it out of the freezer while nobody was looking. For a party or buffet, this super-rich dessert may also be presented in a large soufflé dish, allowing your guests to take just a spoonful in combination with an assortment of other holiday sweets.

ৎঌ

Makes 12 four-ounce ramekins

For the Molds

12 four-ounce porcelain or glass soufflé cups

2 sheets parchment paper or waxed paper

Scotch tape

Soufflés

1 cup sugar

½ cup water

6 egg yolks

½ tablespoon freshly grated nutmeg

½ teaspoon ground cinnamon

¼ cup bourbon

2 tablespoons brandy

2 tablespoons rum

2 cups heavy cream

Garnishes

1 cup roughly chopped toasted pecans

Freshly grated nutmeg

For the Molds

1. Cut the parchment paper (or waxed paper) lengthwise into 2-inch strips.

2. Wrap a paper strip around the outside of the soufflé cup to make a collar extending 1½ inches above the top edge of the dish. Use Scotch tape to secure the paper.

3. Repeat with the remaining ramekins.

For the Soufflés

1. In a small saucepan over medium-high heat, combine the sugar with ½ cup of water. Bring to a boil and continue cooking until the sugar thickens and registers 240 to 246 degrees on a candy thermometer (the "softball" stage). Remove from heat.

2. Meanwhile, place the egg yolks, nutmeg, and cinnamon in the bowl of an electric mixer fitted with a wire whisk attachment. Turn the mixer on and slowly whip the egg yolks on medium speed until they begin to thicken and form a ribbon. Slowly and carefully pour the hot sugar syrup onto the yolks in a thin stream with the motor running. When all of the sugar has been added, continue to whip the yolks on high speed until they are room temperature and very thick. Add the bourbon, brandy, and rum, and beat until just combined.

3. Place the heavy cream in a medium-size mixing bowl. Beat with a wire whisk until it forms soft peaks when the whisk is lifted from the bowl. Using a rubber spatula, gently fold the whipped cream into the egg-yolk mixture.

4. Divide this mixture among the ramekins, filling them almost to the top of the paper collars.

5. Freeze at least 6 hours or overnight.

To Serve

1. Remove the parchment-paper collars and roll the sides of the soufflés in toasted pecans.

2. Store in the freezer until ready to serve.

3. Grate a sprinkling of nutmeg on each soufflé just before serving.

Frozen White Chocolate and Pistachio Terrine

So few gorgeous desserts taste as good as they look — this one tastes even better. The combination of pistachios and white chocolate ice cream is fabulous.

Our talented pastry team worked for months perfecting this, and it has become one of our most popular desserts. For birthdays and anniversaries we form it into a miniature square chocolate box and wrap it in a gilded marzipan bow. It's presented under a caramel dome and cut in half at the table, revealing yet another surprise — a green-and-white checkerboard interior.

Obviously this recipe will take some time to prepare, but it can all be done in stages well in advance, even days before you plan to unveil it to the astonishment of your guests. Ideal for a special occasion, it can be sliced at the table while your friends marvel at how you managed to make the two ice creams into a checkerboard pattern.

℘

Serves 16

Pistachio Ice Cream

2½ cups milk

1 cup heavy cream

¾ cup sugar

¼ cup toasted chopped pistachios

7 egg yolks

2 tablespoons pistachio paste
(available in specialty shops and some gourmet stores)

White Chocolate Ice Cream

6 ounces white chocolate, chopped

1½ cups milk

3 cups heavy cream

½ cup sugar

3 whole eggs

2 teaspoons vanilla extract

2 teaspoons rum

For the Pistachio Ice Cream

1. Line a cookie sheet with plastic wrap and place it in the freezer.

2. In a 4-quart heavy-bottomed saucepan, combine the milk, cream, sugar, and chopped pistachios over medium heat. Bring the mixture to a boil and remove from heat.

3. Place the egg yolks in the top of a double boiler or in a large stainless steel bowl and slowly whisk in the hot cream mixture. Set the mixture over a pot of simmering water and stir until the mixture thickens enough to coat the back of a spoon.

4. Remove from heat, add the pistachio paste, and strain through a fine mesh sieve.

5. Chill in the refrigerator, then freeze in an ice cream machine according to the manufacturer's instructions.

6. Spread the ice cream onto the lined cookie sheet and freeze.

For the White Chocolate Ice Cream

1. Line a cookie sheet with plastic wrap and place it in the freezer.

2. Place the white chocolate in a double boiler or large stainless steel bowl and melt it over a pot of barely simmering water.

3. In a 4-quart heavy-bottomed saucepan, combine the milk, cream, and sugar over medium heat. Bring to a boil and remove from heat.

4. Place the eggs in the top of a double boiler or in a large stainless steel bowl and slowly whisk in the hot cream mixture. Set the mixture over a pot of simmering water and whisk until the mixture thickens enough to coat the back of a spoon.

5. Remove from heat and strain through a fine mesh sieve. Stir in the melted white chocolate, vanilla, and rum.

Continued on page 206

6. Chill in the refrigerator, then freeze in an ice cream machine according to the manufacturer's instructions.

7. Spread the white chocolate ice cream onto the lined cookie sheet and freeze.

Cake

Nonstick cooking spray

5 eggs

6 tablespoons sugar

6 ounces semisweet chocolate, melted

2 tablespoons plus 1 tablespoon (for dusting) all-purpose flour

Pinch of salt

For the Cake

1. Line a 15½ x 10½-inch baking sheet with aluminum foil, smoothing out any wrinkles with a kitchen towel. Spray the foil with a thin coating of non-stick cooking spray. Dust with the flour, tapping the back of the pan to remove any excess.

2. Preheat the oven to 350 degrees.

3. Separate the eggs. Reserve the egg whites. Place the yolks and sugar in the bowl of an electric mixer and whisk on high speed until the yolks are lemon yellow and fluffy, about 5 minutes. Whisk in the melted chocolate, scraping down the sides of the bowl with a rubber spatula to incorporate thoroughly.

4. Using a rubber spatula, fold the flour into the chocolate mixture.

5. In a medium-size bowl, whisk the egg whites until they begin to foam. Add the salt and continue whisking until the egg whites form medium peaks.

6. Gently fold the egg whites into the chocolate mixture, being careful not to overmix. Pour the batter into the prepared pan, smoothing the batter into the corners with a rubber spatula.

7. Bake for 5 minutes. Remove from the oven and let the cake cool in the pan.

Chocolate Ganache Coating

1 cup heavy cream

12 ounces finely chopped semisweet chocolate

For the Chocolate Ganache Coating

1. In a small saucepan, bring the cream to a boil and remove from heat.

2. Place the chocolate in a food processor and, with the motor running, carefully pour in the hot cream in a steady stream. Continue to process for another minute until the chocolate coating is completely smooth.

3. Pour the chocolate coating into a bowl and let cool at room temperature.

To Assemble the Terrine

2 cups ground pistachios

To Assemble the Terrine

1. Invert the pistachio ice cream on top of the white chocolate ice cream and peel off the plastic wrap.

2. Cut the two layers of ice cream in half lengthwise and place one half on top of the other, making four layers. Return the ice cream to the freezer until thoroughly frozen.

3. Cut the layers of ice cream lengthwise again into ½-inch strips. Invert every other strip, forming a checkerboard pattern. Gently press the strips together to close any crevices. Return the ice cream to the freezer until thoroughly frozen again. Wrap the ice cream in plastic wrap and freeze overnight until the ice cream is solid. You will have one checkerboard-patterned block of ice cream that measures approximately 15½ inches in length, 5 inches in width, and 2 inches in height.

4. Remove the frozen block of ice cream from the freezer and place it in the center of the cooled cake. With the edges of the foil used to line the cake

pan, carefully lift the sides of the cake up and wrap the cake around the block of ice cream on the remaining 3 sides.

5. Using the foil, lift the cake-wrapped ice cream out of the pan and invert it onto a wire rack placed on top of a cookie sheet. Carefully remove the foil. If the ice cream is softening, place it in the freezer until it is firm.

6. Pour the chocolate coating over the cake and let it drip down the sides to completely cover the cake on 3 sides. Quickly press the ground pistachios into the chocolate coating and freeze until ready to serve.

To Serve

Slice the terrine into 16 slices and garnish with Blackberry Puree, whole blackberries, and pistachios.

Garnishes

1 cup Blackberry Puree (see below)

1 pint blackberries

¼ cup whole pistachios

Blackberry Puree

This fresh blackberry sauce requires no cooking and has an ideal consistency. If you find yourself with a bumper crop of perfect berries, this sauce can be frozen in small containers for a taste of summer all year round.

1. Puree the berries in a food processor. Strain through a fine mesh sieve to remove the seeds, pressing hard on the solids with a rubber spatula to release all the liquid.

2. Add the lemon juice and mix well.

3. Add the sugar, 1 tablespoon at a time, tasting after each addition, until the desired sweetness is obtained.

Makes 1 cup

3 pints fresh blackberries

1 tablespoon fresh lemon juice

3 to 4 tablespoons sugar

Panna Cotta Parfaits with Red Fruit Jelly

When my friend and colleague Michel Roux, the chef and founder of the Waterside Inn (one of only three Michelin three-star restaurants in England), came over to visit, we composed a very British menu in his honor. It included his own red fruit jelly, which was featured in his newest cookbook. It tasted like summer in the English countryside and also evoked childhood memories of the pleasures of Jell-O.

We layered his red fruit jelly with our favorite panna cotta in a parfait glass and created a stunning make-ahead dessert. While the recipe suggests red currants, cherries, strawberries, and raspberries, any combination of these fruits will work. This is a whimsical resurrection of Jell-O and how it coulda, woulda, shoulda, oughta taste in a grown-up world.

ℰↃ

Serves 8

Red Fruit Jelly

1½ cups red currants, fresh or frozen

1½ cups halved and pitted cherries, fresh or frozen

1½ cups strawberries, stemmed

1½ cups raspberries

3 whole star anise

1 strip orange zest

½ cup sugar

½ cup cold water

1¼ cups cranberry juice

2½ teaspoons powdered gelatin

1 tablespoon fresh lemon juice

Panna Cotta

3 cups heavy cream

1 cup milk

¾ cup sugar

1 vanilla bean, split lengthwise

½ teaspoon powdered gelatin

To Assemble the Parfaits

8 tall champagne flutes or parfait glasses

Garnishes

8 sprigs red currants or raspberries (for garnish)

To Make the Red Fruit Jelly

1. Strip the red currants off their stems.

2. In the top of a double boiler or in a large stainless steel bowl, combine the red currants, cherries, strawberries, raspberries, star anise, orange zest, sugar, and water and cover tightly with plastic wrap. Set the mixture over a pot of simmering water and cook for about 40 minutes.

3. Meanwhile, place the cranberry juice in a small bowl and sprinkle the gelatin over it. When the gelatin has softened, place the bowl over a small pot of simmering water until the gelatin has completely dissolved.

4. Stir the dissolved gelatin mixture into the warm red fruit mixture. Strain through a fine mesh sieve. You should have 2½ cups of strained juice. If you have less, add more cranberry juice. Cool mixture to room temperature.

To Make the Panna Cotta

1. In a 4-quart saucepan, combine the cream, ½ cup of the milk, the sugar, and vanilla bean. Bring to a boil and remove from heat.

2. Place the remaining ½ cup of milk in a small bowl and sprinkle the gelatin over it. When the gelatin has softened, place the bowl over a small pot of simmering water until the gelatin has completely dissolved.

3. Stir the dissolved gelatin mixture into the hot cream mixture, cool to room temperature, and remove the vanilla bean.

To Assemble the Parfaits

1. Carefully fill each of 8 parfait glasses one quarter full with the cooled fruit liquid and refrigerate until set.

2. Pour an equal layer of the liquid panna cotta mixture on top of the chilled fruit jelly and refrigerate until set.

3. Pour another layer of fruit liquid into each glass and refrigerate until set.

4. Finally, fill each glass with a final layer of the panna cotta mixture and refrigerate until ready to serve.

To Serve

Serve the parfaits garnished with sprigs of red currants or raspberries.

Pantry

ℰↃ

½ pound (2 sticks) lightly salted butter

Brown Butter

1. In a heavy skillet over medium heat, melt the butter, stirring constantly.
2. Increase the heat and continue stirring as the butter foams and begins to turn golden brown.
3. Immediately remove the butter from the heat and carefully pour it into a heat-proof container.

∞

Makes I cup

I tablespoon rice wine vinegar

7 tablespoons nuoc mam (fermented fish sauce, available in Asian markets as Vietnamese Nuoc Mam)

2 tablespoons sugar

½ cup cold water

Juice of I lime

2 tablespoons finely julienned carrot

¼ cup minced fresh cilantro

2 large cloves garlic, peeled and minced

2 jalapeño peppers, ribs and seeds removed, finely chopped

Clear Fish Sauce with Lime and Cilantro

1. Mix all the ingredients together in a medium-size bowl, stirring until the sugar is dissolved.
2. Store in the refrigerator until ready to use.

∞

Makes about 1½ cups

2 quarts vegetable or peanut oil (for deep-frying)

½ cup collard-green leaves, washed, thoroughly dried, large stems removed, and cut into very thin strips

Salt to taste

Crispy Collard Greens

Collard greens are easier to deep-fry than spinach or parsley because their leaves are thicker. You can fry them up to eight hours in advance. The fried collards turn emerald green and provide a pleasant crunch. They're fun to nibble on and add an intriguing taste, texture, and appearance to many fish dishes.

1. In a deep fryer or heavy pot, heat the oil to 350 degrees.
2. Add the collard greens to the hot oil, turning them frequently with a skimmer or slotted spoon. Fry just long enough to make them curl, about 30 seconds. Using a slotted spoon, remove the collards from the oil and drain them on paper towels. Sprinkle with salt.

∞

Crispy Fried Onions

1. In a deep fryer or heavy pot, heat the oil to 350 degrees.
2. Dredge the onion rings in flour quickly and shake off any excess.
3. Add the onion rings to the hot oil, turning them frequently with a skimmer or slotted spoon until they just turn golden brown, about 30 seconds. Using a slotted spoon, remove the onion rings from the oil and drain them on paper towels. Sprinkle with salt.

Makes about 2 cups

2 quarts vegetable or peanut oil (for deep-frying)

1 Spanish onion, sliced into paper-thin rings

1 cup all-purpose flour

Salt to taste

Frizzled Leeks

1. In a deep fryer or heavy pot, heat the oil to 350 degrees.
2. Add the leeks to the hot oil, turning them frequently with a skimmer or slotted spoon. Fry just long enough to make them curl, about 30 seconds. Using a slotted spoon, remove the leeks from the oil and drain them on paper towels. Sprinkle with salt.

Makes about 1 cup

2 quarts vegetable or peanut oil (for deep-frying)

½ cup finely julienned leeks, washed and thoroughly dried

Salt to taste

Herbed Potato Crisps

1. Preheat the oven to 300 degrees.
2. Peel the potatoes and place in a pan of cold water.
3. In a medium-size saucepan, heat the butter slowly until melted. Skim off the foam and ladle the clear butter into a small saucepan, avoiding the milky residue in the bottom of the pan.
4. Pour a thin layer of butter on a baking sheet and place in the oven.
5. Remove the potatoes from the water and dry them. Slice them crosswise into ¹⁄₁₆-inch-thick rounds. (Slices will be almost transparent.)
6. Lay half of the potato slices on the hot baking sheet, place one parsley leaf in the center of each slice, and place another slice of potato on top. Brush the top slice with butter and return to the oven.
7. Turn the crisps over with a spatula when they begin to brown on the edges. When the crisps are an even golden brown, remove from the oven and drain on paper towels.
8. Sprinkle lightly with salt while still warm. The crisps may be layered between paper towels, wrapped tightly, and stored for several days at room temperature.

Makes about 12 crisps

2 large Idaho potatoes

½ pound (2 sticks) lightly salted butter

12 fresh parsley leaves

Salt to taste

Makes 1 cup

1 container (4 ounces) mascarpone
  cheese, softened

2 tablespoons mayonnaise

½ cup prepared horseradish

½ cup heavy cream

½ tablespoon kosher salt

Horseradish Cream

1. In the bowl of an electric mixer, combine all of the ingredients.
2. With the mixer on low speed, stir until combined.
3. Whip on high speed for 1 minute. The sauce will thicken a bit. The cream can be made about a day ahead of time and kept in the refrigerator.

Makes 6 tomatoes

6 fresh Italian plum or Roma tomatoes

¼ cup olive oil

1 tablespoon kosher salt

6 fresh basil leaves (optional)

Oven-Roasted Plum Tomatoes

1. Preheat the oven to 200 degrees.
2. Using a sharp-tipped paring knife, core the tomatoes. Place in a small bowl and toss with oil and salt. If desired, stuff a basil leaf into the center of each tomato.
3. Lay the tomatoes on a rack in a small roasting pan and bake for about 4 hours, or until the skins crack and blister. The tomatoes should have a slightly charred appearance.

To Serve

Cool the tomatoes, then remove the basil leaves. Peel, quarter, or halve the tomatoes and use as you would fresh ones.

To Store

Pack the tomatoes closely in a jar or plastic container and cover with extra virgin olive oil. Herbs and garlic may be added to the oil to enhance the flavor.

Makes about 1 pound

3 eggs

2 egg yolks

1½ teaspoons salt

2 tablespoons olive oil

2½ cups all-purpose flour

Pasta Dough

This dough is simple to make, provided you have a pasta machine. The texture of fresh pasta is incomparable and certainly worth the effort for homemade ravioli.

1. In a small bowl, whisk the eggs, egg yolks, salt, and olive oil together.
2. Place the flour in the bowl of an electric mixer fitted with a dough hook. With the mixer on low speed, slowly add the egg mixture in a steady stream. Mix until the dough pulls away from the sides of the bowl and forms a ball. The dough should be slightly wet and elastic. Dust the ball of dough with flour, wrap it in plastic wrap, and refrigerate until ready to use. (The dough can be made in advance and frozen.)
3. Using a pasta machine, roll out the dough and cut it into the desired shape.

Pickled Cranberries

These effortless little pickles make a perfect garnish for roast goose, pork, duck, ham, or turkey and add a festive touch to holiday martinis. Pickled Cranberries can be kept for several months in the refrigerator. They actually improve with age.

1. In a 4-quart saucepan, combine all of the ingredients and bring to a rolling boil.
2. Remove from heat and allow to cool.
3. Discard the cinnamon stick. Pack the cranberries into sterile decorative glass jars or plastic containers. Cover with the cooking liquid and seal.

Makes 3½ cups

1 bag (12 ounces) fresh cranberries, washed and picked over

1¼ cups sugar

1¼ cups apple cider vinegar

½ cup apple cider

½ cup water

5 whole cloves

¼ teaspoon whole allspice

¼ teaspoon black peppercorns

1 whole cinnamon stick

1 teaspoon peeled and roughly chopped fresh ginger root

Pickled Okra

If you've never been able to figure out what to do with okra, try pickling it. It's a terrific garnish for a Bloody Mary and fun to eat with crab cakes. This is a delightful way to preserve garden-fresh okra all year round.

1. In a large stainless steel pot, bring the vinegar, water, sugar, spices, and salt to a boil.
2. Add the okra and return the mixture to a boil. Remove from heat and let cool.
3. Pack the okra pickles into sterile glass jars or airtight containers and fill the jars with the cooking liquid. Add a few sprigs of dill and cilantro to each jar and chill until ready to serve.

Makes 1 quart

1¼ cups white wine vinegar

1¼ cups water

⅓ cup sugar

2 teaspoons dill seed

1¼ teaspoons coriander seed

1¼ teaspoons fennel seed

1¼ teaspoons celery seed

1¼ teaspoons white peppercorns

1¼ teaspoons salt

1 pound okra, tops trimmed

4 sprigs fresh dill (2½ inches long)

4 sprigs fresh cilantro (2½ inches long)

Pickled Red Onions

These simple-to-make pickled red onions are great to have on hand. They add an unexpected piquant garnish to everything from a platter of smoked salmon to a hamburger.

1. In a large saucepan, combine all of the ingredients except the onion and bring to a boil over high heat.
2. Pack the onions into a sterile glass jar or heat-proof container. Pour the boiling liquid over them. Allow to cool to room temperature. Cover tightly and refrigerate. The Pickled Red Onions can be made well in advance and stored in the refrigerator until ready to use.

Makes 3 cups

1 cup red wine vinegar

½ cup sugar

½ bay leaf

2 whole allspice berries

1 whole star anise

2 whole cloves

2 medium-size red onions, halved and thinly sliced

Pizza Dough

1½ teaspoons dry yeast

1½ cups warm water

2 tablespoons olive oil

4¼ cups all-purpose flour

2½ teaspoons salt

1. In a large mixing bowl, dissolve the yeast in the warm water.

2. Whisk in the olive oil and 2¼ cups of the flour. Cover with a tea towel and let rise 1½ hours.

3. Stir in the remaining flour and the salt.

4. Turn the dough out onto a floured board and knead for 4 to 5 minutes, or until the dough is smooth and elastic.

5. Let the dough rest for 10 minutes before rolling.

Red Pepper Coulis

Makes about 1 quart

2 sprigs fresh parsley

2 sprigs fresh thyme

1 bay leaf

1 piece of cheesecloth (about 10 inches square)

1 twelve-inch length of kitchen string

5 red bell peppers, cored and seeded

½ cup chopped carrot

1 cup chopped onion

½ cup chopped celery

2 cups Vegetable Stock (see page 221) or water

3 dashes Tabasco

Salt, freshly ground black pepper, and sugar to taste

1. Place the parsley, thyme, and bay leaf in the center of the cheesecloth square, draw up the corners to form a little bundle, and tie it closed with the string, making a sachet.

2. In a medium-size saucepan over high heat, combine the peppers, carrot, onion, celery, herb sachet, and Vegetable Stock and bring to a boil. Simmer until the vegetables are completely tender, approximately 20 minutes. Remove and discard the sachet.

3. Puree the mixture in a blender or food processor and strain through a fine mesh strainer. If the coulis is too thin, pour it into a saucepan and simmer over low heat until it thickens slightly.

4. Season with Tabasco, salt, pepper, and sugar. The coulis may be made a day in advance and stored in the refrigerator.

Red Wine Butter Sauce

Makes 1¼ cups

1 cup balsamic vinegar

1⅛ cups red wine

1 shallot, peeled and sliced in half

¼ cup (½ stick) cold, unsalted butter, cut into tablespoon-size pieces

½ cup (1 stick) cold, lightly salted butter, cut into tablespoon-size pieces

1. In a medium-size heavy-bottomed saucepan, combine the vinegar, wine, and shallot over medium heat and reduce to a syrupy consistency.

2. Reduce the heat to low and, piece by piece, stir in the unsalted and salted butter with a wooden spoon, incorporating one piece of butter before adding the next. When all of the butter is incorporated, remove the shallot pieces.

3. Add the salt and pepper. Keep the sauce warm (not hot) until ready to serve.

Note: It used to be thought that this sauce could not be held for any length of time, but fortunately that myth has been debunked. It keeps nicely in a stainless steel canister resting in a water bath at 125 degrees for several hours. Some clever home cooks hold it in a thermos on the back of the stove. Be aware that if it becomes too hot or too cold, it may separate and look like plain old melted butter instead of the satiny sauce it's meant to be. If you find yourself the victim of this misfortune, here's a little trick for bringing the sauce back. Simply bring 3 tablespoons of heavy cream to a boil in a small saucepan and reduce for a few minutes until syrupy. Remove from the heat and gradually whisk the "broken" sauce into the cream; the sauce will regain its lustrous consistency.

&

Roasted Garlic

1. Preheat the oven to 350 degrees.
2. Toss the garlic in the oil and wrap in aluminum foil. Roast for 25 minutes. Remove from oven and allow to cool to room temperature.
3. Peel the garlic and mash it in a mortar or with a fork in a small bowl.

Makes about 1 tablespoon

10 cloves garlic, unpeeled
1 teaspoon olive oil

&

Roasted Red Pepper

1. Char 1 large red bell pepper over an open flame or broil in the oven until blackened on all sides.
2. Wrap the pepper in aluminum foil and cool for 30 minutes. This allows the pepper to "sweat," making it easier to peel.
3. Peel, split, and seed the pepper.

1 large red bell pepper

&

Roasted Tomato and Shallot Fondue

1. Preheat the oven to 350 degrees.
2. Lay the shallots in a small, shallow, oven-proof baking dish and pour the oil over them to a depth of ½ inch. Cover the dish with aluminum foil or a lid and bake for 1 hour, or until the shallots are soft.
3. When the shallots are cool enough to handle, peel off the skin and squeeze out the flesh. Coarsely chop the shallot flesh and the roasted tomatoes. Combine in a medium-size bowl. Add the vinegar, salt, and pepper. Mix well and place in a Pyrex baking dish about 2 inches deep. Press the bay leaves and thyme sprigs into the mixture. (If using dried thyme, stir it in.)
4. Bake, uncovered, for about 15 minutes, or until slightly thickened. Stir occasionally to prevent a crust from forming.
5. Remove fondue from the oven. Discard the bay leaves and thyme sprigs.

Salt and freshly ground black pepper to taste

Serves 8

12 whole fresh shallots, unpeeled
Olive oil
24 Oven-Roasted Plum Tomatoes (see page 214), peeled
2 tablespoons balsamic vinegar
Salt and freshly ground pepper to taste
2 bay leaves
2 sprigs fresh thyme or 1 teaspoon dried

&

Makes 3 cups

2 tablespoons Dijon mustard

½ tablespoon chopped shallot

½ teaspoon minced garlic

1½ tablespoons dry sherry

⅔ cup sherry vinegar

1 cup salad oil

⅔ cup olive oil

¼ cup walnut oil

Salt and freshly ground black pepper
   to taste

Sherry Vinaigrette

1. Whisk all the ingredients together in a large stainless steel bowl. Transfer to a jar with a tight-fitting lid.

2. Store in the refrigerator and shake well or whisk thoroughly before using.

ℰ

Makes 2 quarts

9 cups water

4 cups sugar

Simple Syrup

1. Combine the water and sugar in a heavy-bottomed saucepan over medium heat. Stir until the sugar is completely dissolved and the liquid is clear. Remove from heat and cool to room temperature.

2. Store indefinitely in the refrigerator.

ℰ

Makes 3 quarts

10 pounds very ripe tomatoes

6 large cloves garlic, peeled and
   smashed

1 four-inch piece ginger root, sliced

4 sprigs fresh rosemary

4 sprigs fresh thyme

1 piece of cheesecloth (about 10
   inches square)

1 twelve-inch length of kitchen string

2 tablespoons vegetable oil

2 large Vidalia onions, sliced

Salt and freshly ground black pepper
   to taste

Stewed Gingered Tomatoes

When tomatoes are plentiful and at their peak of flavor, this is a good way to put some aside for the winter. The texture of these tomatoes is improved by pureeing a portion of them and mixing the puree with the quartered, stewed tomatoes. A bit of ginger root, fresh rosemary, and thyme combine to add interest and a depth of flavor to this Southern staple.

1. Bring a large pot of water to a boil. Plunge the tomatoes into the boiling water for 10 seconds and remove them with a slotted spoon. Cut out the stems and peel off the skins. Quarter the tomatoes and set aside.

2. Place the garlic, ginger root, rosemary, and thyme in the center of the cheesecloth square, draw up the corners to form a little bundle, and tie it closed with the string, making a sachet.

3. Heat the oil in a large soup pot over medium heat. Add the onions and cook them for 5 minutes, or until they are soft and translucent.

4. Add the tomatoes and the sachet. Lightly season with salt and pepper, and simmer over low to medium heat for 20 minutes, stirring occasionally.

5. Remove the sachet and season the tomatoes with celery salt, salt, and pepper.

6. Whisk the cornstarch and water together in a small bowl and add it to the tomatoes. Return to a simmer and remove from heat.

7. In a blender, puree one third of the stewed tomatoes and combine them with the remaining tomatoes in the pot.

8. Pour the stewed tomatoes into sterile glass jars and can, freeze, or refrigerate until ready to serve.

1 teaspoon celery salt

2 tablespoons cornstarch

½ cup cold water

Sweet-and-Sour Fish Sauce

Makes about 1½ cups

1 cup sugar

½ cup rice wine vinegar

⅓ cup tomato juice

2 teaspoons fresh lemon juice

1 tablespoon nuoc mam (fermented fish sauce, available in Asian markets as Vietnamese Nuoc Mam)

1. In a 1-quart saucepan, combine the sugar and vinegar. Cook over medium-high heat until the mixture turns amber in color and then remove the saucepan from the heat.
2. Slowly and very carefully whisk in the tomato juice. Whisk in the lemon juice and the nuoc mam. This sauce can be made up to 5 days in advance, stored in the refrigerator, and rewarmed before serving.

ഉ

Tarragon Vinaigrette

Makes 2 cups

1 teaspoon dry mustard

2 tablespoons minced fresh tarragon or 1½ teaspoons dried tarragon

½ teaspoon minced garlic

½ teaspoon chopped shallot

1 teaspoon salt

1 tablespoon fresh lemon juice

2 teaspoons raspberry vinegar

⅓ cup red wine vinegar, preferably imported

1 cup extra virgin olive oil

Freshly ground black pepper to taste

1. Whisk all the ingredients together in a large stainless steel bowl. Transfer to a jar with a tight-fitting lid.
2. Store in the refrigerator and shake well or whisk thoroughly before using.

ഉ

Tempura Batter

Makes about 2 cups

1 cup cake flour

7 ounces very cold club soda

Salt and freshly ground black pepper to taste

After years of experimenting with every tempura batter imaginable, we finally discovered that, oftentimes, simpler is better. This recipe uses only soda water, flour, salt, and pepper. Fine-textured soft-wheat flour, packaged as cake flour, makes a more delicate tempura, but regular flour will suffice.

1. Using a fork, gently combine the flour and club soda in a small bowl. (The batter will appear slightly lumpy and should have the consistency of heavy cream.)
2. Season with salt and pepper to taste. (The bubbles in the soda water help keep the tempura light and crispy; therefore, it is important to make the batter just before using it.)

ഉ

Tomato Vinaigrette

1. In a food processor fitted with the blade attachment, combine the tomato, white wine vinegar, tomato paste, egg yolk, salt, and sugar until smooth.
2. With the motor running, add the olive oil in a thin stream.
3. Strain through a fine mesh sieve. The vinaigrette may be made in advance and stored in the refrigerator until ready to serve.

෨

Makes about 1 cup

1 ripe tomato, cored

2 tablespoons white wine vinegar

1 tablespoon tomato paste

1 egg yolk

2 teaspoons kosher salt

1 teaspoon sugar

1/4 cup extra virgin olive oil

Vegetable Stock

1. Place all of the ingredients except the salt in a stockpot over high heat and cover with cold water. When the stock comes to a simmer, skim off any foam or residue that rises to the surface.
2. Simmer for 30 minutes.
3. Remove from heat and allow to steep for 45 minutes.
4. Strain the stock and season with salt. Let cool to room temperature and refrigerate.

Note: The flavor of the finished stock can be intensified by bringing it to a boil and reducing it over high heat. Vegetable stock may be frozen.

෨

Makes about 1 quart

2 cups coarsely chopped carrots

2 cups coarsely chopped onion

2 cups coarsely chopped celery

1 bay leaf

1 tablespoon whole black peppercorns

4 sprigs fresh thyme

4 sprigs fresh parsley

Salt to taste

Waffle Potato Chips

You will need a mandoline to cut the potatoes into a waffle shape. The chips can be made in advance and stored in an airtight tin. These gaufrette *chips, as the French call them, add a flair to any sandwich.*

1. In a deep fryer or heavy pot, heat the oil to 350 degrees.
2. Peel and shape the potatoes into neat ovals and place them in a bowl of cold water until ready to use.
3. With the ruffled blade of a mandoline adjusted to make ¼-inch-thick slices, cut one potato at a time crosswise into rounds, turning a quarter turn after each slice so that one side of the slice is ruffled horizontally and the other side is ruffled vertically.
4. Rinse the slices in cold water to prevent discoloration. Pat them dry on paper towels.
5. Carefully slip the potatoes into the hot oil, turning them frequently with a skimmer or slotted spoon, and fry for 2 to 3 minutes until they are golden brown. Using a slotted spoon, remove the chips from the oil and drain them on paper towels. Sprinkle with salt.

෨

Makes about 24 chips

2 quarts vegetable or peanut oil (for deep-frying)

2 Idaho potatoes

Salt to taste

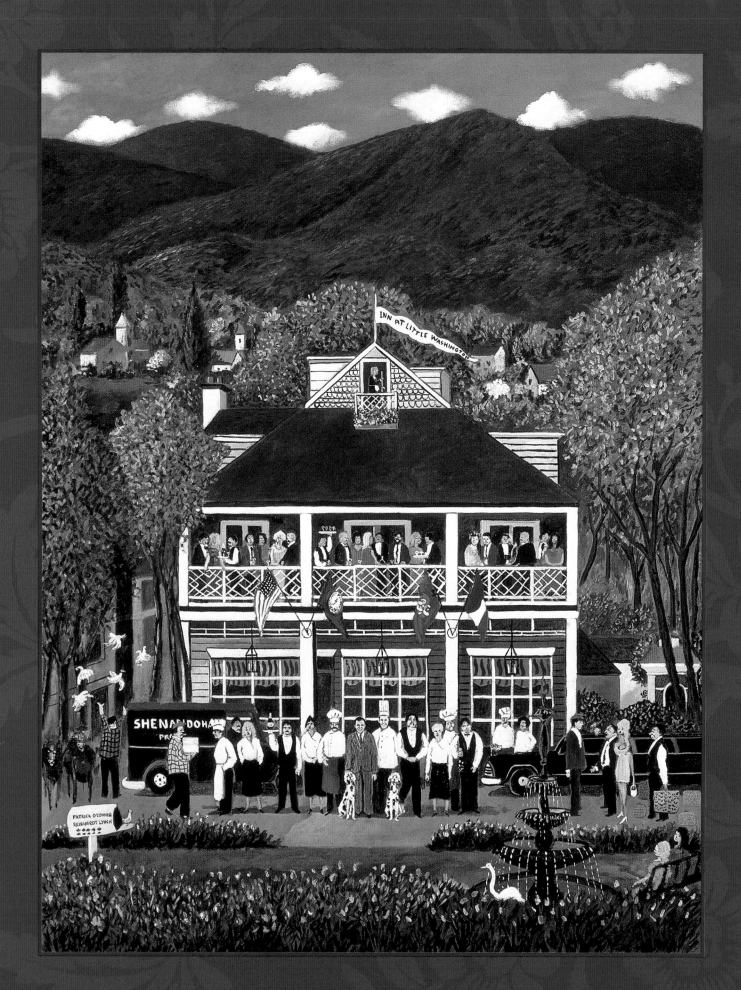

A Brief History of
The Inn at Little Washington

๙๑

Long, long, ago and far, far away, in a tiny town nestled deep in the foothills of the Blue Ridge Mountains, sixty-seven miles away from its big-sister city on the Potomac, the 158 inhabitants of "Little" Washington watched with amusement and incredulity as two long-haired young men set about converting a former garage on the corner of Main and Middle streets into a restaurant.

The barnlike frame-and-stucco building was constructed around 1895 and had operated as a gas station with a dance hall above it. Wrecked cars still decorated the side yard. The structure had been a candidate for demolition, but it was deemed too expensive to tear down and too risky to burn — given its location. *Who do they think is cummin'?* was the question most of the townfolk were asking themselves as they watched the construction taking place in their midst.

Years earlier, the town had been bypassed by a new four-lane highway, so travelers no longer drove through it on their way to Shenandoah National Park and points beyond. Most tourists didn't even know Little Washington existed as they sailed past going sixty miles an hour. The town's economy had plummeted. The filling stations dried up and withered on the vine. Young people began moving away and looking for work elsewhere.

Patrick O'Connell and Reinhardt Lynch had been operating a catering business out of an old unheated farmhouse nearby, using a wood-burning cookstove and an electric frying pan. After a few years, they had developed a small following of well-to-do clients in desperate need of a local eatery.

The partners were able to rent the old garage in town for $200 a month. With a savings of $5,000 between them and a loan from a nearby bank, they were able to build a kitchen and begin transforming the old building into a charming country restaurant.

The Inn at Little Washington opened on January 28, 1978, during the worst blizzard of the decade, with no liquor license, insufficient electrical power, and a staff of three. Weeks afterward, a Washington,

D.C., restaurant reviewer dined anonymously and wrote that it was the best restaurant in a radius of 150 miles of the nation's capital. The cheapest entrée was $4.95.

At the end of the first year, the partners closed for the month of January and went on a gastronomic pilgrimage to the great restaurants of France. At that time there were few destination restaurants outside major metropolitan areas to use as role models within the United States, and these European reference points became instrumental in galvanizing a direction and in shaping an ultimate goal for The Inn at Little Washington to achieve.

O'Connell had not received any formal training as a chef, and it was particularly inspirational for him to meet several of the greatest chefs working in Europe at the time and to realize that they were also self-taught. These winter forays to Europe's best restau-

rants became a yearly tradition, and when plans for overnight accommodations at the Inn began to take shape, the partners also began visiting the world's best hotels.

By 1984, The Inn's first guest rooms opened to glowing reviews from the travel press. In 1987, The Inn became a member of the Paris-based luxury hotel association Relais & Châteaux and, in 1989, made history when it became the first inn ever to receive Mobil Travel Guide's Five-Star Award. The press had a field day. *USA Today* did a three-page color spread.

A year later, Mobil announced that The Inn had received two Five-Star Awards — one for its restaurant as well as one for the accommodations — marking the first time in Mobil's thirty-four years of rating hotels and restaurants that an establishment had won two awards simultaneously.

The Inn at Little Washington remains a life's work in progress.

ℰℛ

Celebrities, politicians, and hospitality leaders flocked to Little Washington to see what on earth was going on.

Success built on success. In 1991, the James Beard Foundation began honoring American chefs at its annual galas. The second year, O'Connell was named Best Chef in the Mid-Atlantic Region. The next year, The Inn was recognized as the Outstanding Restaurant in America and went on to win national awards for service and wine service. Then, in 2001, Patrick was honored with the prestigious Outstanding Chef in America Award.

Year after year, The Inn is rated number one in all categories by Zagat's *Washington, D.C., Restaurant Survey*. The *International Herald Tribune* picked The Inn as one of the ten best restaurants in the world, and *Travel + Leisure* magazine rated The Inn number one in North America and number two in the world in its World's Best Awards.

O'Connell and Lynch seem to thrive on challenge — not the least of which is living up to the impossible expectations that so many accolades engender. Fortunately, they consider this to be their opiate. They like to think it keeps them young.

The Inn at Little Washington remains a life's work in progress.

Index

&

Additional Photo Credits

۶۵

The letter following each page number refers to the position of the photograph on the page (L=left; R=right; T=top; M=Middle; B=bottom).